Muslim-Christian Dialogue

Islamic Monotheism vs. Trinity

By Jalal Abualrub

Edited by Alaa Mencke

Madinah Publishers and Distributors
ISBN: 978-0-9856326-5-6
www.IslamLife.com; Info@IslamLife.com

Madinah Publishers and Distributors
ISBN: 978-0-9856326-5-6
www.IslamLife.com; Info@IslamLife.com

1

Table of Contents

Chapter One: Islamic Monotheism vs. Trinity

This is a Muslim-Christian dialogue pertaining to the essence of the Islamic faith as compared to Christianity. In this book, we will keep the identity of the Christian questioner anonymous, but will narrate his arguments intact for the benefit of the readers, except for the parts that will be discussed in subsequent booklets, Allah willing. We also reorganized our response, and added more benefits and references, so as to offer our readers the maximum benefit.

What is the *Kalimah*?

The Christian questioner asks, "My point is simply that the Kalima is not found in one verse in the Quran as such. It is made up of multiple verses, just like the Trinity. So why should the same principle, that a theological teaching is founded on multiple verses, only be acceptable in Islam but not in Christianity? I am not talking about the Sunnah because it is of less value then the Quran among Muslims and they cannot agree among each other as to which one is authentic. If you want to talk about the Sunnah in this regard then I will talk about the Christian equivalent, the writings of the early church fathers. They very clearly spell out the Trinity and all the other doctrines of Christianity. Regarding the 99 names of Allah. Do Shias not believe in them? If they do then my point is like the one above: Two of his names are not found in the Quran."

The Islamic *Kalimah*

In one *ayah* (Quranic statement), Allah says, {*Know* (O, Muhammad) *that Lâ ilâha illallâh* (none has the right to be worshipped but Allâh), *and ask forgiveness for your sin, and also for* (the sin of) *believing men and believing women.*}

This *ayah* establishes the Islamic *'Kalimah'* in just one sentence. However, I do not truly know what the questioner means by *'Kalimah'* and where he got it from. If the questioner means by *'Kalimah'* the Islamic Monotheism, the word of *Tau'heed, Kalimat-u At-Taqwa,* then, here it is in one *ayah, ayah* 47:19 above.

Two more *ayat* from the Quran, Islam's holy book:
1. {*Allâh! Lâ ilâha illa Huwa* (none has the right to be worshipped but He), *Al-`Hayy-ul-Qayyum* (the Ever-Living, Who sustains and protects all that exists). *Neither slumber nor sleep overtakes Him. To Him belongs whatever is in the heavens and whatever is on the earth. Who is he that can intercede with Him except with His Permission?*

He knows what happens to them (His creatures) *in this world, and what will happen to them in the Hereafter. And they will never compass anything of His Knowledge except that which He wills. His Kursî* (literally a footstool or chair) *extends over the heavens and the earth, and He feels no fatigue in guarding and preserving them. And He is the Most High, the Most Great.}* (2:255)

2. *{Follow what has been revealed to you* (O, Muhammad) *from your Lord, Lâ ilâha illa Huwa* (none has the right to be worshipped but He) *and turn aside from Al-Mushrikûn* (polytheists, those who worship others beside Allah)} (6:106).

This is the testimony of Monotheism as sent to Prophet Muhammad, Allah's Messenger, whose job was to convey it to mankind and to seek forgiveness for the believers from Allah, Who owns forgiveness.

Why can't Christianity bring a clear verse, only one, plainly explaining and declaring their Trinitarian creed as the creed to follow? Just one verse from the Old Testament, the New Testament, or words from Jesus that establish the Trinitarian creed similar to the Quranic method of establishing its monotheistic *Tau'heed* creed in clear terms in one sentence each.

Instead, the usual habit of Christians is to collect various texts scattered throughout their holy books then conclude the following, "This verse means this, that verse means that, add them together and there you have it: Trinity." They glue together 'interpretation' of different texts then claim that the meaning supports their creed.

In contrast, *La Ilaha illallah*, the *Kalimah*, the foundation of Islam, is found throughout the Quran, why can't Christians bring a single verse that clearly speaks of their creed without vagueness or the need for complex interpretation? Even multiple verses that **clearly** identify Trinity as the correct creed such as in the words of Jesus, will do. Christendom does not have that. They have multiple interpretations and corruption of texts, even Old Testament texts. Meanwhile, the Jews, who wrote the Old Testament with their own hands, vehemently reject Christian claims as to the true meaning of the texts Christians use to support Trinity.

As soon as he was commanded, Prophet Muhammad declared this to his people, **"O, My People! Say, 'La ilaha illallah' and you will become successful."** (*Al-Badr Al-Munir*, by Ibn al-Mulaqqin, 1/680)

The First Commandment in the Words of Jesus

The words reported from Jesus also use the Islamic *Kalimah* as the one and only correct creed, *"The first of all the commandments is, Hear, O Israel; The Lord our God is one Lord. And thou shalt love the Lord thy God with all thy heart, and with all thy soul, and with all thy mind, and with all thy strength: this is the first commandment."* (*Mark* 12:29-30)

This is **not** Trinity. This is the Islamic *Tau'heed*, and as such, constitutes clear proof against Christianity. Jesus never said, "I created you; worship me like you worship God; I am one in three and three in one; I am God, really." All what Christians have are vague statements that they gather together then fight with each other –endlessly- as to what they truly mean.

Therefore, the conflict here is not between the Islamic *Tau'heed* which is mentioned in one or multiple Quranic statements, versus Trinity which is also mentioned in multiple versus in the Bible. The conflict is between Quranic statements that establish its creed versus a creed that is not mentioned in the Bible in individual or multiple verses.

Chapter Two: Status of Muhammad's Sunnah

As for Prophet Muhammad's Sunnah, who among Muslim sects does not accept the Sunnah? Not even Shi`as outright say they reject Prophet Muhammad's Sunnah; they know that, no doubt, to reject the Sunnah means to become a disbeliever.

All Muslims accept the Sunnah as the resource of Islam along with the Quran. Disbelievers are those who claim to be Muslim yet defy the entire *ummah* (nation) of Muhammad, peace be on him, by rejecting his Sunnah, especially since the Quran ordains obedience to it. Allah said, {*It is not for a believer, man or woman, when Allâh and His Messenger have decreed a matter that they should have any option in their decision. And whoever disobeys Allâh and His Messenger, he has indeed strayed into a plain error.*} (33:36)

More than 90% of Muslims are now as they have been throughout the history of Islam, *Sunnis*. 'Sunnis' accept Prophet Muhammad's Sunnah (a hint: this is why they are called 'Sunnis' to begin with).

The questioner's statement that Muslims cannot agree on what is authentic, is profoundly false, even bizarre. Sunni Muslims agree on the *Two Sahihs*, Bukhari's and Muslim's, as the most authentic books after the Quran. These two are the most reliable *hadeeth* and Sunnah collections Muslims have.

Muslims also agree on most other *hadeeths* found in the major resources of Sunnah. Sunni Islam is the original Islam, not only the majority group among Muslims. Muslims take their practices and code of conduct from the Sunnah.

The questioner might have been reading for offshoot sects that claim to be Muslim, such as the *Quranis*. This minor and deviant sect only accepts the Quran, so they can explain the Quran as their hearts desire. Yet, proving their blatant hypocrisy, they have to use the Sunnah to practice aspects of Islam that are not found in the Quran. Major scholars of Islam consider this sect to be out of the folds of Islam.

Or, the questioner may be referring to certain *hadeeths* that Muslims disagree on pertaining to the authenticity of the chains of narration that report them. However, this is not because the Sunnah is of lesser value to the Quran, but the opposite, because the Sunnah is divine. Consequently, Muslims make it their mission to distinguish between what is established and what is not established with regards to the Prophet's statements and actions. In other words, *the rejected hadeeths are rejected precisely because it has been proven that the Prophet did not say them.*

In all religions, there are people who invent stories and statements and ascribe them to their respective prophet or leader. Hypocrites, liars, those who have weak faith, non-Muslims who pretended to be Muslim, ignorant Muslims, also invented statements then ascribed them to the Prophet of Allah, Muhammad, peace be on him.

However, Muslims, in contradiction to all other religions, have established the scientific *isnad* method. Here is a segment from the book titled, ***Muhammad's Role in Islam***, "To preserve the integrity of the Sunnah and the Quran's practical *Bayan* (explanation), Muslim Scholars devised an outstanding and scientifically precise method of protecting the Prophetic Tradition from corruption. It is called the method of, '*Isnad*,' meaning, using chains of narrators to establish the validity, or lack thereof, of any statement or action attributed to the Prophet." (***Muhammad's Role in Islam***, Jalal Abualrub, Pg., 101)

Contrary to the questioner's claim, Muslims agree on most *hadeeths* that establish Islam in its various aspects. The Sunnah is practiced by Muslims on a daily basis and is emphasized by scholars in lectures, classes, and during Friday speeches. The Sunnah is the Muslim law; it has thousands of details and rulings that entail and encompass aspects of life and religion.

Sunnah rulings govern the affairs of Muslims pertaining to acts of worship, dealings, transactions, behavior and code of conduct, family affairs, including marriage and divorce, and judicial, economic and educational aspects. Muslims have been living the Sunnah for more than 14 centuries. *Muslims have been marrying for more than 14 centuries according to the Sunnah, since the Quran does not have the intricate details of such aspects.*

12

It is a rather bizarre claim that the questioner makes about the Sunnah being less than the Quran, when in fact Muslims use details of the Sunnah in their lives more so than details about life and religion found in the Quran. This is because the Quran contains mainly general guidelines, while the Sunnah contains the intricate details that explain the general guidelines in the Quran.

The questioner, and all others who are not familiar with Islamic topics, can simply ask any Sunni Muslim, even youngsters, about the Sunnah and they will attest to it being the resource of Islam along with the Quran. Just say to any Muslim these words 'Bukhari and Muslim,' and they will attest to their being the second and third most authentic books in Islam after the Quran. Further, the generation that preserved the Quran from corruption is the very generation that protected the Sunnah from corruption. They reported both and preserved both.

In the Quran, Allah declares the Sunnah as a revelation, {*Nor does he* (Prophet Muhammad) *speak of* (his own) *desire. It is only a Revelation revealed.*} (53:3-4). In the Quran, Allah orders Muslims to take the Sunnah as a judge, {*But no, by your Lord, they can have no Faith, until they make you* (O, Muhammad [his Sunnah]) *judge in all disputes between them, and find in themselves no resistance against your decisions, and accept* (them) *with full submission*} (4:65).

Thus, the Quran itself declares the Sunnah as a part of the revelation. Therefore, for the questioner to try and exclude the Prophet who came with the Quran from being the authority to explain it is not only rejected, but also plainly false. For the questioner to state that the Sunnah is of lesser value than the Quran is directly contradicted by the Prophet who was sent with the Quran, who said, *"I was given the Quran and its equal with it* (i.e., the *Sunnah*)" (A *Sahih* (authentic) *hadeeth*; *Al-Hadeethu `Hujjatun bi-Nafsihi*).[1]

They Are Not 'Equivalents'

The Sunnah is the tradition of the Prophet who was sent with the Quran, i.e., the very same man, Muhammad, peace be on him. The Sunnah was duly recorded in the same method and by the same generation as the Quran was.

Early Trinitarian Christian elders, in contrast, are not Jesus or the authors of the numerous books contained within the New Testament. They are anonymous, unknown regarding identity and trustworthiness, never met Jesus or his disciples, and never accompanied the authors of the New Testament books. According to Christian authorities (as quoted

---

1 [Albani, Muhammad Nasir ad-Deen. *Al-Hadeethu `Hujjatun bi-Nafsihi fi-l-A`hkami wa-l-`Aqa-id* (The *Hadeeth* is Proof Itself in Matters of Law and Creed) (Pg., 26-27). (Allah blessed this author to translate this book into English.)]

in this book), true early Christian elders did not propagate Trinity.

Therefore, the Sunnah and early Trinitarian Christian traditions are not, cannot possibly be equivalent to each other.

Prophet Muhammad came with the two resources, the Quran and the Sunnah which he taught to thousands of his companions, male and female. The Quran, the Muslim holy book, is the Literal Word of Allah. The Sunnah is the divine explanation of the Quran formed by the words and actions of the Prophet himself, as the Quran states, {*And We have also sent down unto you* (O, Muhammad) *the Dhikr* (the Qur'ân), *that you may tubayyina* (give the *bayan*, meaning, explain clearly) *to men what is sent down to them, and that they may give thought*} (16:44). How Muslims pray is not specified in the Quran, but in the explanation of it called the 'Sunnah.'

In contrast, Jesus came with none, neither the New Testament nor other early Christian writings. Early Trinitarian Christian writings were not authored by those who authored the New Testament or those who authored early Christian writings. Early Christian writings were authored decades, even centuries after Jesus departed from this earth, alive and well, but before the advent of Trinity into Christianity in the fourth century.

Therefore, there are four different resources to consider here:

1. **Jesus preached the Injil:** "*And Jesus went about all Galilee, teaching in their Synagogues, and preaching the Gospel of the kingdome*" (**Matthew** 4:23).
   This book no longer fully exists in any language.

2. **New Testament books:** Jesus never saw, authored or authorized any of these books, which were written decades, even centuries after Jesus was ascended to heaven, alive. These books also no longer fully exist in their original form.

3. **Early Christian writings:** These writings were compiled by unknown authors of unknown trustworthiness.

4. **Early Trinitarian Christian writings:** These writings were inserted into Christianity in the 4th century CE.

Thus, the comparison is severely deficient. On one hand, both the Quran and Sunnah were taught, explained and practiced by the Prophet who was sent with them, in his lifetimes and under his supervision. The Quran is Muhammad's Quran who was sent with it from Allah, the Sunnah is Muhammad's Sunnah who was sent with it from Allah; Muslims have perfect record of both resources.

In comparison, the New Testament does not contain the Gospel of Jesus. It was not written by him, or authorized by him, nor did he see any of their authors with his own eyes. The early Trinitarian teachers and writers developed their creed in the 4th century. Had they had a single Trinitarian Gospel or clear biblical verses that establish Trinity, they would not have needed to forge such a creed in the 4th century. Instead, Trinity would have been present and proclaimed since the time of Jesus, if it were a true creed.

Many Literal Words of God

The questioner seems to forget that most Christians are Catholic and Orthodox; they have entire extra books in their holy Bible that are rejected by smaller cults, such as the Protestants. Using his logic, the Catholic Bible is of a lesser value as evidence since Christians cannot agree on what is authentic in it or not. This is a far cry from Muslims disagreeing on certain *hadeeth* reports that are not established by authentic chains of narration, which means the Prophet did not say them to begin with.

Chapter Three: The 99 Names of Allah

One needs to be consistent: where exactly is the text that establishes the 99 names of Allah? The *hadeeth* that lists the 99 names is not established according to the major scholars of Sunnah, such as Imam at-Tirmidhi. It is a weak, rejected *hadeeth*, not because it is not found in the Quran, but because it is not established by authentic chains of narration.

In other words, Muslims know that the Prophet did not say this *hadeeth*. This *hadeeth* was rejected by Muslim scholars themselves and as such is not part of the Sunnah. The 99 names of Allah are not listed in the Quran or the authentic Sunnah in one sentence or paragraph. This topic is also irrelevant to our discussion. In addition, since the questioner discounts the status of the Sunnah as compared to the Quran, it is strange that he would use a statement that is not found in the Quran to begin with.

Islamic Prayer Described

All Muslims pray in the manner they pray based on the Sunnah that reached them; the Quran does not teach how to pray. For instance, and to assert these facts, one can visit any *masjid* (falsely called 'mosque') in the world, no matter the country or the sect, during times of prayer. One will then find that all Muslims in that *masjid* pray behind one Imam (literally: leader), and that they pray the same number of *rak`ah* units all other Muslims offer in every other *masjid*. If one then searches the Quran, one will not find in it instructions on how to perform the prayer, Islam's most important practical pillar.

This, indeed, is a magnificent demonstration of the power of the Sunnah. The Quran contains the order to pray in many *ayat*, such as, {*And they were commanded not, but that they should worship Allâh, and worship none but Him Alone* (abstaining from ascribing partners to Him), *and perform As-Salât* (*Iqâmat-as-Salât* [establish Prayer perfectly and on time]) *and give Zakât* (obligatory Alms), *and that is the right religion*} (98:5). However, the Quran does not specify how to pray; the Sunnah does where the Prophet ordered Muslims to, *"Pray as you have seen me pray"* (*Sahih Al-Bukhari* 680).

To Muslims, the Quran and the Sunnah are the same. To Muslims, the Quran and the Sunnah are a revelation. To Muslims, the Quran and the Sunnah complete each other. Muslims agree on the vast majority of *hadeeths* found in the most authentic resources, such as *hadeeth* compilations of Imams Bukhari, Muslim, Abu Dawud, At-Tirmidhi, An-Nasaii, Ibn Majah, A'hmad Ibn Hanbal, Malik Ibn Anas, and so forth.

Shi`a vs. Mormons

What the Shi`as believe or do not believe is not relevant, because our discussion is on the sources of Islam not what various Islamic sects believe. Yet, even the Shi`a generally pray as Sunnis do, even though how to pray is not found in the Quran but in the Sunnah.

We will not hold the questioner or his brand of Christianity responsible for the ideas and practices of other Christian sects, such as Unitarians, Mormons, Jehovah's Witnesses, who state that there are 50,000 mistakes in the Bible, Maronites, Copts, Amish, and so forth, who may disagree with major aspects of the questioner's faith. Further, the author of these answers, Jalal Abualrub, is not a Shi`a, but follows the mainstream Muslim majority that was established during the Prophet's time and continues to be a majority until this day, the Sunnis.

Christian *Kalimah*

The questioner writes, "You (Jalal) asked: 'Where is the clear unequivocal text in your book that Jesus is lord, or the son of god, or one in three and three in one, or anything like this at all?' Well, here it is. I copied it from an article found on (www.christianityexplained.net.tc): **Evidence that Jesus is God in the flesh from the sayings of Christ :** *'I tell you the truth,' Jesus answered, 'before Abraham was born, I am!' (John 8:58)* In this way Jesus expresses his oneness with God and the eternity of his being. By saying **'I am'** *(Greek: 'ego eimi')* and not **'I was', Jesus is using the personal name by which God revealed Himself in the Old Testament! The first translation of the Old Testament into Greek between the third and first century BC, known as 'Septuagint' uses the words 'ego eimi' in Isaiah 41:4, 43:10 and 46:4 to refer to God. (See also Isaiah 43:25, 45:6, 51:12, 52:6)."**

Here is the list of Old Testament verses the questioner used to prove the divinity of Jesus as pertains to *'Ego Eimi* (I AM).' What is astounding is that in all of the instances where 'I AM' is mentioned here, 'I AM' is explained by the context. None of these texts says, 'I AM,' alone. Each of these texts has 'I AM' describing something else before or after.

I used the English Standard Version of the Bible here, written in simple English, so that the reader can -as I did- read these verses as many times as possible to find out if *'Ego Eimi'* stands alone without something to explain what it means, and if it alone pertains to the personal name of God.

1. *"Who has performed and done this, calling the generations from the beginning? I, the LORD, the first, and with the last; I am he."* (**Isaiah** 41:4)
   'I AM he,' here is explained by *"Who has performed and done this..."*

2. *"You are my witnesses, declares the LORD, and my servant whom I have chosen, that you may know and believe me and understand that I am he. Before me no god was formed, nor shall there be any after me."* (**Isaiah** 43:10)
   'I AM he,' is explained by *"Before me no god was formed, nor shall there be any after me."*

3. *"I, I am he who blots out your transgressions for my own sake, and I will not remember your sins"* (**Isaiah** 43:25).
   'I AM,' is defined by *"...he who blots out your transgressions."*

4. *"That people may know, from the rising of the sun and from the west, that there is none besides me; I am the LORD, and there is no other"* (**Isaiah** 45:6).
   Here, 'I AM,' is explained by *"...the LORD, and there is no other."* In addition, *"There is none besides me,"* defeats Trinity every time.

5. *"Even to your old age I am he, and to gray hairs I will carry you. I have made, and I will bear; I will carry and will save."* (**Isaiah** 46:4)
   'I AM he,' is defined by, *"I will carry you ... I will carry and will save."*

6. *"I, I am he who comforts you; who are you that you are afraid of man who dies, of the son of man who is made like grass"* (**Isaiah** 51:12).
   'I AM,' continues with, *"he who comforts you."*

7. *"Therefore my people shall know my name. Therefore in that day they shall know that it is I who speak; here am I."* (**Isaiah** 52:6)
   'AM I,' is explained by, *"...it is I who speak."*

Not a single '*Ego Eimi*' quoted here qualifies as anything without the complete sentence that explains it. Not a single '*Ego Eimi*' quoted here qualifies as anyone's name, let alone being God's personal name. How '*Ego Eimi*' is used to prove the divinity of Jesus is as much a mystery as Trinity itself.

Pure Monotheism

Allah revealed Himself in the Quran, and His Prophet described Him in the Sunnah, in the clearest of terms, as follows.

Allah said in the Quran, {*Say* (O, Muhammad): *"Who is the Lord of the heavens and the earth?" Say: "(It is) Allâh." Say: "Have you then taken* (for worship) *Auliyâ'* (protectors) *other than Him, such as*

23

have no power either for benefit or for harm to themselves?" Say: "Is the blind equal to the one who sees? Or darkness equal to light? Or do they assign to Allâh partners who created the like of His creation, so that the creation (which they made and His creation) *seemed alike to them?" Say: "Allâh is the Creator of all things; and He is the One, the Irresistible."}* (13:16)

Allah's Prophet said in the Sunnah, *"Whoever testifies that none has the right to be worshipped but Allah, Alone Who has no partners, and that Muhammad is His Slave and Messenger, and that Jesus is Allah's Slave and Messenger and His Word which He bestowed on Mary and a Spirit created by Him, and that Paradise is true and Hell is true, Allah will admit him into Paradise with the deeds he had done even if those deeds were few"* (*Bukhari* 3180, and, *Muslim* 41).

These statements are plain, clear, simple and magnificent in any language; they do not need interpretation in any language.

In contrast, what the questioner presents here with regards to Jesus being God, is as much a mystery as Trinity itself. For instance, 'I AM,' with capital letters (remember that Greek does not have capital vs. lower case letters as English does), is hardly proof for Trinity or divinity. *'I AM,' by itself, does not have a meaning in any language.*

Among the most bizarre aspects of Christian methods in describing God as being a community of three, is that they bring texts that establish the oneness of God in the strict numerical sense of the word, to prove that He is three. For instance, the questioner quotes a verse from the Old Testament where, Christians claim, God says [in Greek!], '**ego eimi**,' to prove that Jesus is god. Yet, the verse where that statement is made discusses the oneness of God in clear terms, *"See now that I, even I, am he, and there is no god with me: I kill, and I make alive; I wound, and I heal: neither is there any that can deliver out of my hand"* (***Deuteronomy*** 32:39). Note that the Old Testament was not written in Greek. Therefore, '**ego eimi**,' is a translation from an unknown original. 'I AM,' is a translation of yet another translation.

Deuteronomy 32:39 in no way speaks of a community of gods. Is it possible that '*there is no god with me*,' would in any language mean, 'there are two other gods with me; We are a community of three'? Is it possible that anyone would overlook the fact that 'I AM' is defined by '*there is no god with me*'?

Is not ***Deuteronomy*** 32:39 similar to the statement Prophet Ibrahim (Abraham), peace be on him, made about the description of Allah, {***And recite to them the story of Ibrâhîm*** (Abraham). *When he said to his father and his people: "What do you worship?" They said: "We worship idols, and to them we are ever devoted." He said: "Do they hear you, when you call on* (them)? *Or do they benefit you or do they harm* (you)?" *They said: "(Nay) but we found our fathers doing so." He said: "Do you observe that which you have been worshipping, you and your ancient fathers, verily, they are enemies to me, save* the Lord of the 'Âlamîn (all that exists). *Who has created me, and it is He Who guides me. And it is He Who feeds me and gives me to drink. And when I am ill, it is He Who cures me. And Who will cause me to die, and then will bring me to life* (again). *And Who, I hope, will forgive me my faults on the Day of Recompense* (Day of Resurrection).} (26:69-82)

The power and beauty of Allah's Islamic Monotheism and the wonderful way Allah's Prophets describe Him cannot escape the attention of those who look at a text and understand the exact opposite of it.

Why Not Adam, Heaven and Earth?

Why would Jesus compare himself to Abraham, instead of Adam? He should have said, "Before Adam, heavens and earth, I was (or I AM)." Why the vagueness?

This statement, 'I AM,' only declares to the Children of Israel that Jesus is their prophet. He is letting them know that, even though they invoked the name of Abraham but not his character or piety as Jesus often said to them, he is their particular prophet, not Abraham. If this statement really came from Jesus, then it would mean, "I am your Prophet, not Abraham." Or, Jesus only meant to say, "Before Abraham was born, I was a prophet," meaning, Allah designated Jesus as a prophet in His eternal knowledge, before Abraham was born, as is the case with all other prophets.

What agrees to this meaning are the words he said two verses before, *"Your father Abraham rejoiced at the thought of seeing my day; he saw it and was glad."* The meaning mentioned here is also supported by this translation for, ego eimi: *"Before Abraham was born I was already what I am"* (*The Twentieth Century New Testament*, Fleming H. Revell Company).

Amusingly, and faced by the tremendous differences between Christians themselves on the meaning of, ego eimi, some fanatical Protestant evangelicals dismiss other translations for this concept, because it did not come from their version of Christianity. Yet, most Christians do not consider Protestants to be true Christians to begin with. Since Protestant translations and creed are being dismissed by most Christians, why should we adopt their view on what the New Testament means as compared to other versions of Christianity?

The most amusing part that has escaped Christians, and some Muslim authors who respond to them, is that Christian sects are disputing with each other over a translation of a translation of a supposed original that does not exist. There is no doubt that Christendom cannot prove that Jesus said ego eimi in any language, because they have no access to his original statement.

The prophets are foretold about the prophets to come after them, especially if they are from among their descendants, so they can give the glad tiding to their people about their coming. Similarly, the Quran states that Prophet Jesus, peace be on him, informed the Children of Israel about Prophet Muhammad's coming, {*And when 'Îsâ* (Jesus), *son of Maryam* (Mary), *said: "O, Children of Israel! I am the Messenger of Allâh unto you, confirming the Taurât* [(*Torah*) which came] *before me, and giving glad tidings of a messenger to come after me, whose name shall be Ahmad* (one of the names of Prophet Muhammad). *But when he* (A'hmad, Muhammad) *came to them with clear proofs, they said: "This is plain magic."*} (61:6)

Christians, in contrast, can never find what Jesus truly said, because they cannot find the original copy of any of his statements or of any book contained in the Bible. '**Ego eimi** (I AM)' for instance, was inserted in the New Testament in its Greek form. What was the original word Jesus spoke in his native language? Had Christians had it, they would have produced it rather than inserting words into their holy books in a language foreign to Jesus. Jesus, peace be on him, never spoke Greek or Latin, and never preached the Gospel in Greek or Latin. It is said that he spoke Aramaic. The Old Testament was never originally written in Greek or Latin, either.

There are considerable differences between Christians pertaining to '**Ego eimi**' and how it should be translated. There is no doubt that translating it as 'I AM' is a 'preference' for some Christians; it is not a clear divine text that can only carry one meaning. Those who inserted this word into the New

Testament carry the burden of their wicked act. They busied Christians for hundreds of years, and added more confusion to the confusion they already have about major aspects of their religion.

Yet, we will leave this matter to Christians and Jews to solve their disputes about this and other religious aspects. But just to make a point: to many Christians, *"Before Abraham was born I was already what I am,"* competes with their preferred meaning for, *"ego eimi."* What if these two statements do not compete, but actually complement each other? In this case, it would only mean that Jesus was referring to God's knowledge that he will be a prophet even before Abraham was born. Christians have no proof for any other meaning.

Chapter Four: *'Ego Eimi'*

If the readers do a simple search on the Internet for **'Ego eimi,'** they will enjoy, as I do, the way Christians and Jews debate with each other on what these words mean and how they should be translated. The amusing part is that while they all struggle with each other about which translation is more accurate, they do not discuss the most important question, "Who wrote the original, in what time frame, what guarantee does anyone have that what they wrote is accurate?"

Christians vs. Aramaic Bible

Interestingly, Christians have trouble accepting the Aramaic copy of the Bible. This is how those who wrote the Aramaic Bible wrote *John* 8:58, *"Timeless truth I speak to you: Before Abraham would exist, I AM THE LIVING GOD."* Christians are just fascinated with using capital letters when they speak of Jesus.

Before the questioner rejoices with the news of this verse, and knowing that Christians in general do not rely on the Aramaic copy of the Bible to begin with, one should investigate the method the Online Parallel Bible (http://bible.cc) reports different translations of *John* 8:58. They use different versions of the Bible to translate every verse, including from Aramaic. The reader will then discover for themselves how Christians cannot agree on even this verse as they translate it differently from each other.

Clearly, the Aramaic version of the Bible has been altered to give a meaning to *John* 8:58 that is not found in any other Gospel. This is proof that the Bible was changed and corrupted. Otherwise, how can the Aramaic Bible alone and in contradiction to all other versions of the Bible report this outrageous statement ascribed to Jesus? Obviously someone inserted these words as evident from the fact that all other versions do not have *"I AM THE LIVING GOD"* whether in capital letters or lower case letters.

What is more astounding than all of this, is the fact that Christians think that Jesus is, "**God in the flesh.**" Yet, this supposed God in the flesh could never clearly say, "I AM GOD." Instead, he says something vague that keeps Christians busy for millenniums while trying to interpret its meaning. He also runs away in fright from the Jews, his own creation -as Christians tell us, as they try to stone him, *"Then took they up stones to cast at him: but Jesus hid himself, and went out of the temple, going through the midst of them, and so passed by."* (*John* 8:59). This story demeans God to no end; it is false in every respect.

Christendom has no access to the original statement Jesus made here or anywhere else in the New Testament; they have to rely on translations on non-existent original manuscripts, which in turn, are unknown regarding authenticity and true origin.

31

Chapter Five: Western Encyclopedias on Trinity

In, *50 Righteous and Humane Concepts Brought by Muhammad*, under Title, '*Wa-Shahida Shahidun min Ahliha*' (A Witness of Her Own Household Bore Witness'), the author writes, "Major Western encyclopedias and dictionaries, written in the Christian West, by mainly Western Christians, admit to these facts:

The New Encyclopedia Britannica: 'Neither the word Trinity nor the explicit doctrine appears in the New Testament, nor did Jesus and his followers intend to contradict the Shema in the Old Testament: 'Hear, O Israel: The Lord our God is one Lord' (Deuteronomy 6:4). ... The doctrine developed gradually over several centuries and through many controversies. ... It was not until the 4th century that the distinctness of the three and their unity were brought together in a single orthodox doctrine of one essence and three persons. ... By the end of the 4th century ... the doctrine of the Trinity took substantially the form it has maintained ever since.'

The Encyclopedia Americana: 'Christianity derived from Judaism and Judaism was strictly Unitarian [believing that God is one person]. The road which led from Jerusalem to Nicea was scarcely a straight one. Fourth century Trinitarianism did not reflect accurately early Christian teaching regarding the nature of God; it was, on the contrary, a deviation from this teaching.'

The Columbia Encyclopedia: 'Trinity ... the doctrine is not explicitly taught in the New Testament.'

The New Catholic Encyclopedia: 'The formula [one God in three Persons] itself does not reflect the immediate consciousness of the period of origins; it was the product of 3 centuries of doctrinal development. ... The formulation 'one God in three Persons' was not solidly established, certainly not fully assimilated into Christian life and its profession of faith, prior to the end of the 4th century. But it is precisely this formulation that has first claim to the title *the Trinitarian dogma*. Among the Apostolic Fathers, there had been nothing even remotely approaching such a mentality or perspective.'

Encyclopedia of Religion and Ethics: 'In the New Testament we do not find the doctrine of the Trinity in anything like its developed form, not even in the Pauline and Johannine theology.'

Encyclopedia International: 'The doctrine of the Trinity did not form part of the apostles' preaching, as this is reported in the New Testament.'

New Bible Dictionary: 'The word Trinity is not found in the Bible, and, though used by Tertullian in the last decade of the 2nd century, it did not find a place formally in the theology of the Church till the 4th century.'

Dictionary of the Bible: 'The trinity of God is defined by the Church as the belief that in God are three persons who subsist in one nature. The belief as so defined was reached only in the 4th and 5th centuries AD and hence is not explicitly and formally a biblical belief.'

New International Dictionary of New Testament Theology: 'The NT does not contain the developed doctrine of the Trinity ... primitive Christianity did not have an explicit doctrine of the Trinity such as was subsequently elaborated in the creeds of the early church.'

The Oxford Companion to the Bible: 'Because the Trinity is such an important part of later Christian doctrine, it is striking that the term does not appear in the New Testament. Likewise, the developed concept of three coequal partners in the Godhead found in later creedal formulations cannot be clearly detected within the confines of the canon. ... While the New Testament writers say a great deal about God, Jesus and the Spirit of each, no New Testament writer expounds on the relationship among the three in the detail that later Christian writers do." (*50 Righteous and Humane Concepts Brought by Muhammad*, Jalal Abualrub, Pg., 20-22)

Thus, the texts to prove Trinity the questioner quotes are not agreed upon by Christians, to truly say the least. Had there been clear texts to prove Trinity, Christians would have celebrated them and shown them to the entire world. Instead, they have to invent an elaborate scheme to prove what does not exist in

34

the Bible. They twist and corrupt texts and glue together what may mean a host of things, then claim that Trinity exists in the Bible.

It has been an amusing journey that this author went through while challenging Christian preachers, evangelicals, theologians, and teachers, to ponder on what western encyclopedias -written by Christians- are telling them in the clearest terms: **Trinity, the creed, is not in the Bible.** Instead, Christian preachers dismiss these encyclopedias and persist in the practice of gluing together various biblical sentences to form a creed out of them. It seems that they think they have a monopoly on Christianity and Christian ideology: it is 'their version' that is true as compared to everyone else's.

Next, the questioner quotes a long article by Dr. James White, which will be addressed in another booklet following this one, Allah willing.

On the *Kalimah* Again

The questioner continues, by writing, "My answers to your comments are found ... below. Please post them on your website too. ... The word 'kalima' is the Muslim declaration of faith (see: http://www.geocities.com/fearallaah/kalimahs.htm the first one is the most important one in Islam: "There is no diety except Allaah. Muhammad (sallallaahu alayhi wasallam) is the Messenger of

Allaah." My point is simply that neither the first one, nor all the other Kalimas mentioned in the above site, are found in one verse in the Quran as such. They are made up of multiple verses, just like the Trinity. So why should the same principle, that a theological teaching is founded on multiple verses, only be acceptable in Islam but not in Christianity? This will answer you points."

There are many '*Kalimat* (words)' mentioned in the Quran, according to their respective context. What the questioner read on the website he mentioned is not the word of *Tau'heed* divided between various *ayat* where none of them alone describes the foundation of Islam. What he read instead is *Kalimat* collected by the people who run that website for the purpose of teaching, by discussing instances where variances of the word 'word' are used in the Quran.

The topics they collected are as numerous as their respective contexts are, such as this instance, {*And when those who associated partners with Allâh see their* (Allâh's so-called) *partners, they will say: "Our Lord! These are our partners whom we used to invoke besides you." But they will throw back their word at them* (and say): *"Surely, you indeed are liars!" And they will offer* (their full) *submission to Allâh* (Alone) *on that Day, and their invented false deities* [they used to invoke besides Allâh, e.g., idols, saints, priests, monks, angels, jinn, Jibrîl (Holy Ghost),

Messengers (such as Jesus)] *will vanish from them.*}
(16:86-87)

As the questioner correctly stated, the foundation of the Islamic creed is, *'La-ilaha illallah'*; this is the Islamic faith as compared to Trinity and Idol-worship. This is the 'word' that makes one a Muslim if one declares it. This is the 'word' that, if one refuses to declare it, one remains a disbeliever. When the Prophet's uncle was dying, the Prophet offered this word to him, *"Say 'La ilâha illallah,' that I may testify for you with Allah on its account'"* (*Sahih Al-Bukhari* 1360).

The Islamic Faith in One Word

Tau'heed, Allah's Islamic Monotheism, the pillar of the Islamic creed, is found in the Quran in many instances in just one sentence. This is the *'Kalimah'* that Prophet Muhammad was sent with. It means, 'There is no deity worthy of worship, except Allah'. This is the Islamic religion. The Quran said that every prophet who came before Prophet Muhammad also came with this 'word,' {*And We did not send any messenger before you* (O, Muhammad) *but We revealed to him* (saying)*: Lâ ilâha illa ana* [none has the right to be worshipped but I (Allâh)], *so worship Me* (Alone and none else)"} (21:25).

This is the *'Shahadah* (Testimony)' that Allah made in the Quran, {*Allâh bears witness that Lâ ilâha illa Huwa* (none has the right to be worshipped but He), *and the angels, and those having knowledge* (also give this witness); (He always) *maintains His creation in justice. Lâ ilâha illa Huwa* (none has the right to be worshipped but He), *the All-Mighty, the All-Wise. Truly, the religion with Allâh is Islâm. Those who were given the Scripture* (Jews and Christians) *did not differ except, out of mutual jealousy, after knowledge had come to them. And whoever disbelieves in the Ayât* (proofs, verses, signs, revelations, etc.) *of Allâh, then surely, Allâh is Swift in calling to account.}* (3:18-19)

Note how the *Kalimah* of *Tau'heed* is mentioned twice in one *ayah* **followed** by Allah's statement that the religion with Him is Islam.

The *Shahadah*, testimony of *Tau'heed*, Allah's Islamic Monotheism, has always been the same no matter the prophet whom Allah sent. Here is what Prophets Moses and Jesus said about it, *"Hear, O Israel: The Lord our God is one Lord"* (*Deuteronomy* 6:4, and, *Mark* 12:29). Thus, the Old Testament and the New Testament have, in one sentence, what Trinity lacks in hundreds of pages contained in the Old Testament and the New Testament.

Every prophet who was sent came with this *Kalimah*, the foundation of Islam. Also, every prophet who was sent came with another *Kalimah*, the testimony that he is a messenger from Allah. For instance, *'La ilaha illallah; Muhammadun rasulullah'* are two *Kalimat*, not one.

The first *Kalimah* establishes the religion of *Tau'heed*; the second *Kalimah* establishes the prophet who was sent with it, and mainly pertains to the law. The second of these two *Kalimat* changes according to the messenger who was sent. For instance, *'Muhammadun rasulullah,'* is a testimony that one makes, after accepting *Tau'heed*, asserting that one believes in and is dedicated to following Muhammad, the Messenger who was sent to all of humankind until the Day of Judgment.

Chapter Six: The Two Islamic *Kalimat*

The Two Islamic *Kalimat* are also mentioned in one statement in various instances in the Quran, such as, {*Say* (O, Muhammad): *"O Mankind! Verily, I am sent to you all as the Messenger of Allâh — to Whom belongs the dominion of the heavens and the earth. Lâ ilâha illa Huwa* (none has the right to be worshipped but He). *It is He Who gives life and causes death. So believe in Allâh and His Messenger* (Muhammad), *the Prophet who can neither read nor write* (Muhammad), *who believes in Allâh and His Words* (this Qur'ân, the Taurât (Torah) and the Injeel (Gospel)), *and follow him so that you may be guided."*} (7:158)

During the time of Prophet Moses, the two *Kalimat* would have been, '*La ilaha illallah*,' followed by the statement that the Children of Israel were required to make, '*Musa rasulullah*,' because at the time, Musa (Moses) was their Messenger from Allah.

Therefore, I am confused about what the questioner said. Had he made a simple research, he would have easily found the *ayat* quoted above, instead of making an uninformed claim that, Islam does not have its faith in one *ayah*.

We asked the questioner for a clear testimony establishing Christian faith from the Bible through the words of Jesus. Instead of answering our request, the questioner keeps referring to the Two Islamic Testimonials from the Quran thinking that they are the equivalent of what we asked him to produce.

One *Kalimah* or Two *Kalimat*

La ilaha illallah, Muhammadun rasulullah, are called, *Ash-Shahadatan,* meaning, the Two Testimonials, not, the One Testimonial. This is because they are two testimonies, not one. To become Muslim one has to testify to and proclaim both of the Two Testimonials.

What is the opposite/equivalent of Trinity, is it, *Muhammadun rasulullah,* meaning, Muhammad is the Messenger of Allah, or, *La ilaha illallah,* that is, 'None is worthy of worship, except Allah'?

What is the Islamic Creed in few words? The answer would not be, *Muhammadun rasulullah,* but, *La ilaha illallah. La ilaha illallah,* is the Creed on which Islam is founded, while, *Muhammadun rasulullah* identifies the messenger who was sent with it.

Trinity is about the nature, and consequently, the rights of God. It does not compete with, 'Muhammad is the Messenger of Allah,' but rather with, '*La ilaha illallah,*' which asserts that Allah is One. The equivalent of, '*Muhammadun rasulullah,*' is, "*As my Father hath sent me, even so I send you* (the disciples of Jesus)" (*John* 20:21).

Therefore,

1. Jesus came to the Children of Israel with *'La ilaha illallah'*: *"The first of all the commandments is, Hear, O Israel; The Lord our God is one Lord"* (**Mark** 12:29);
2. He also declared that Allah sent him as a messenger to the Children of Israel, *"my Father hath sent me"* (**John** 20:21);
3. And only to the Children of Israel, *"I am not sent but unto the lost sheep of the house of Israel"* (**Matthew** 15:24);
4. The Children of Israel confirmed that Jesus was a prophet, *"And the multitude said, This is Jesus the prophet of Nazareth of Galilee"* (**Matthew** 21:11).

Capital-Lettering

The questioner says, next, "I Am' is translated from the Greek in capital to emphasize the fact that it is a personal name, in this case the same name God uses about Himself in the Old Testament."

We ask the questioner to produce a clear statement **wherein Jesus says**, "I created you; I am God; Worship me as you worship God; I and the Holy Ghost are a part of Trinity; Trinity is your creed; Worship all three of us, the son, the Holy Ghost and the Father, and these three are one god." However, the questioner has not answered our question yet.

What does 'personal name' mean? Where did it say in the Old Testament that 'AM' is the personal name of God and that if anyone uses it, he is also a god? All this is pure conjecture for which there is no shred of proof or evidence.

Simple But Powerful

Muslims believe that Allah never had a son, and they can prove it from the Quran, {*Allâh is* (the only) *One Ilâh* (God), *glory is to Him* (far exalted is He) *above having a son. To Him belong all that is in the heavens and all that is in the earth. And Allâh is All-Sufficient as a Disposer of affairs.*} (4:171)

Muslims believe that there is none worthy of worship, except Allah, and they can prove it from the Quran in one sentence, {*Such is Allâh, your Lord! Lâ ilâha illa Huwa* (none has the right to be worshipped but He), *the Creator of all things. So worship Him* (Alone), *and He is the Wakîl* (Trustee, Disposer of affairs, Guardian) *over all things.*} (6:102)

Muslims believe that Trinity is false, and they can prove it from their Book in one *ayah*, {*Surely, disbelievers are those who said: "Allâh is the third of the three* (in a Trinity)." *But there is no Ilâh* (god) (none who has the right to be worshipped), *but One Ilâh* (God —Allâh). *And if they cease not from what they say, verily, a painful torment will befall on the disbelievers among them*} (5:73).

Can Christians prove their Trinity from the words of Jesus? Even multiple words will do; words that speak of Trinitarian creed in clear terms. Vague statements in Greek or Latin will not provide an answer to this challenge. Jesus never spoke Greek, Latin, German or English. 'I AM' in no language means that one who says it is God. Capital 'AM' is not a name, let alone being a 'personal name'. Certainly, Jesus did not speak in capital letters either.

Next, the questioner quotes one of my comments about Trinity then says, "Also, if Jesus and the Father are one, why did not the Father die when his son died, if they are in perfect harmony as Christians claim?' The answer is found in the definition of the Trinity: **'We worship one God in Trinity, and Trinity in Unity; Neither confounding (mixing up) the Persons; nor dividing the Substance (Essence)'** The word 'Person' is here used in the sense of 'self with a particular function.' ('The Illustrated Bible Dictionary' by F.F. Bruce, IVP Leicester, 1962, see 'person')"

Consequently, Trinity is a mystery! We fully agree. There is no sound explanation for Trinity no matter the Christian believer -who is trying to explain it- and how scholarly in the Bible they may be. The biggest problem that always existed with what the questioner said above is that none of it was ever said by Jesus himself. No part of the explanation the questioner presented here came from the Old Testament or the New Testament. All this is the purely speculative Christian justification for their invented creed. The sentences the questioner gave here can never be found in their holy books.

Disappearance of God and the Holy Ghost

We are told that Trinity is not confounding ('confusing' is a better synonym for 'confounding' than, 'mixing up'). However, when Jesus died, he 'gave up' the Holy Ghost. Obviously they were mixed up, especially since when they separated, there was a consequence for the separation in that one of them died. The separation also annuls the argument that Trinity is not '**dividing the Substance (Essence).**'

Yet, separation did not cause the Holy Ghost to die. This negates the perfect harmony Christians claim exists between the Triune Council, as well as, negating the notion of the three gods always indwelling each other by the fact that a separation between at least two of the gods occurred.

Even then, it seems that 'indwelling' caused two of the three divine beings to be mixed up, resulting in the death of one of them when they separated. Yet, God the Father seems to be nowhere in this rather confusing formula of ever-indwelling, ever-perfect harmony, interrupted by instances of separation, and death, but only for Jesus not for the other two gods.

Jesus is supposed to indwell the Holy Ghost and the Father, forever. Then, Jesus separated from the Holy Ghost, but not from the Father who seems to have had no role in all of this operation. Either the three were not mixed up or they were mixed up. Either the three indwell each other or they don't.

Here it seems the two positions occurred at the same time, as well as, their opposites in that two of the three, Jesus and the Holy Ghost, became separated, no longer indwelled in each other, but two, Jesus and the Father (as well as the Father and the Holy Ghost), still continued indwelling each other. Meanwhile, Jesus had no clue about any of this, because he supposedly protested why the Father (but not the Holy Ghost and not himself) abandoned him, *"Eloi, Eloi, lama sabachthani? which is, being interpreted, My God, my God, why hast thou forsaken me?"* (**Mark** 15:34)

To Confound or not to Confound, that is a Confusing Question

The questioner says, "**...each member of the Godhead in some sense indwells the other, without diminishing the full person hood of each.**"

However, to die, Jesus 'gave up' the Holy Ghost. Thus, the 'Son-self' was diminished by the departure of the Holy Ghost; he died as a result of the discontinuity of coexisting with at least one of the three persons in the Godhead. Yet, God might have simply been forgotten in all of this; there is no mention of Him here, whether He remained indwelled in Jesus or separated Himself from him.

We are told that Trinity is not dividing, i.e., the three gods retain their mutual essence. Yet one of the three died, i.e., lost the very 'essence' of eternal life, while the other two did not die, thus interrupting their mutual essence. Obviously, division occurred, because one of the three became 'separated' from the other two (or at least from one of them) and died. Earlier, another division occurred when one of the three became human. Later, another division occurred when one of the three was resurrected as a human, again.

As for the notion that 'The word 'Person' is here used in the sense of 'self with a particular function,' it contradicts the Christian familiar theme that the Triune council acts in prefect harmony. Here it seems that the questioner is suggesting a separation between the perfect-harmony shared by the three, by claiming that each 'person' has a particular function. These two themes contradict each other.

If the three are in prefect harmony, then the three have a unified action with no distinction between who initiated the action (in which case there is no 'need' for multiplicity to begin with). If the three act separately, then there is no perfect harmony between them. The latter concept is emphasised in the claimed death of one of the three, Jesus, while the other two, God and the Holy Ghost, remained alive and unaffected.

Chapter Seven: Perfect-Harmony vs. Individualism

The explanation of Trinity gets more confusing when the questioner says, next, "The essential unity of the Godhead, then, is found both in their intrinsic equality of divine characteristics and also in the intensely personal unity that comes from mutual indwelling ('The self-giving triune God, the imago dei and the nature of the local church: an ontology of mission', paper by J. Scott Horrell, Th.D, professor of Systematic Theology at Dallas Theological Seminary)."

The concept of Godhead is easy to understand and comprehend. The Old Testament and the Quran, as well as clear statements from Jesus in the New Testament, profess a one God, one nature, one essence, on action, one personality and oneness in creation, commandment and decision.

Trinity Godhead is ever confusing. Here we have one God, but three persons. They are united in divine nature and qualities, but divided in action and even fate. For instance, the job of the Father is different from the job of the Son and the Holy Ghost. Christians assign to each of these personalities different roles, decisions, actions, presence, and consequences of actions and decisions.

To explain, the Son-God is the one who transformed into a man, who lived a human life. This description is not given to the Father or the Holy Ghost, because they did not incarnate as the Son did. When the Son died, he gave up the Holy Ghost, not the Father. If Christians were asked about who among the three became a man, they will not say it was the Father or the Holy Ghost, only the Son. If Christians are asked about who gave up the other, the Holy Ghost or Jesus, they will not say it was the Holy Ghost, but Jesus.

Therefore, Trinitarian Christians assign different roles and different actions to each member of the Triune Council. Yet, they somehow consider the three to be in perfect harmony, then claim that "It has to be stated emphatically that Christians do not worship three gods but one God." However, Christians worship three divine beings, three different partners, three different personalities, three different manifestations, i.e., three different gods.

What is astonishing is that Christians did not find these concepts in their holy books. They invented them. Neither the Old Testament nor the New Testament ever uttered such concepts or notions. This is pure Christian personal interpretation on Trinity.

God's Love for Creation

The questioner says, next, "Thus when God the Son died at the cross, God did not cease to exist but was separated from himself regarding the relationship within the Trinity not regarding his essence. To think that God gave up a perfect relationship for a time shows how great his love towards us is!"

The questioner seems to be confused. God did not give up anything according to the very texts the questioner uses here, which state that it was Jesus who gave up the Holy Ghost. Nowhere in the New Testament does it say that when Jesus died, he gave up the Father as he gave up the Holy Ghost.

Consequently, it would make more sense for the questioner to change his statement as follows, "Thus when God the Son died at the cross, he did not cease to exist but was separated from God the Holy Ghost regarding the relationship within the Twin-ity not regarding his essence. To think that God the Son gave up a perfect relationship with God the Holy Ghost for a time shows how great his love towards us is!"

No doubt, Allah (God), the Holy Ghost, and Jesus have nothing to do with this clear misguidance.

The Changing God

When the Son supposedly temporarily 'gave up' his intensely personal unity with the Holy Ghost, they no longer were bound together with the intensely personal unity, which, we are told, is in the essence of Trinity. The essence of God has thus changed. All three of the Triune Council changed; one died while another, the Holy Ghost, separated from the one who died as a consequence of the separation; meanwhile, the Father may also have separated Himself from the one who died, but not from the one who gave up the one who died. The essence of the relationship has thus changed.

Each of the three gods had 'different functions,' such as Jesus becoming a man while the other two did not. Therefore, where is the intensely personal unity which the three have? Jesus ate food, the other two didn't; so where is the intensely personal unity? Jesus died, but God does not die. Jesus changed, even though the Bible claims he does not change, "*Jesus Christ the same yesterday, and to day, and for ever*" (**Hebrews** 13:8). This statement has no meaning in light of the fact that Jesus was spat on by Jews, smacked by Romans then crucified by some of his creation, so we are told.

The fact is that Jesus never said he is God; it is the Christians who say that. He never uttered such statements, never authorized anyone to utter them on his behalf. No one can truly explain or understand these concepts and God never spoke of them in the Old Testament or the New Testament. How can Christians explain all this unreasonable and unexplainable utter confusion as being '**not contrary to reason**'?

Still a Mystery

The questioner then says, "It is held that although the doctrine is beyond the grasp of human reason, it is, like many of the formulations of physical science, **not contrary to reason, and may be apprehended though it may not be comprehended by the human mind.**' (See, 'Encyclopedia Americana', 'Trinity', by F.C. Grant, Danbury, Con.: Americana Corp., 1980)"

We agree with the questioner that Trinity is beyond the grasp of human reason. This is because it was invented by confused humans who described God as their human minds dictated to them without authority from God or a revelation to guide them. What is farther from human grasp, though, is how all these concepts were invented without consulting with Jesus or with God.

The questioner continues, "The Trinity of God, like many other facts about him does not have to be understood fully, but to be believed in. Faith, the simple childlike trust that God is and acts as he

53

revealed himself in the Bible, is sufficient for salvation. Similarly, one does not have to understand how a Television set works in order to enjoy a program about nature. A simple touch of the right button will bring about the blessing."

The problem is that God never revealed Himself in this way to any of His creation in any of His revelations or by the words of any of His Prophets. Normally, revelation comes first **then** one believes in the doctrine in a simple childlike trust, as the questioner puts it. Here, the doctrine was first developed and then its edicts were forced on the revelation.

The questioner says, next, "It is really interesting how you keep widening the subject. I am more than willing to talk about this allegation. But since you have no time what is the point of doing so?' I just give you one thing to consider: *'Let the People of the Gospel judge by what Allah hath revealed therein. If any do fail to judge by (the light of) what Allah hath revealed, they are (no better than) those who rebel.' (Surah 5, Al Ma'idah, verse 47)* This command is given to Muhammad's contemporaries, it is written in the 'present' tense which in the Arabic language can also refer to the future! If the Gospel (Injil) was corrupted at that time then surely Allah would never have asked the people of the Gospel, the Christians, to believe in it! So the Gospel was OK in the sixth century according to the Quran. To find out whether it is OK in the 21st century existing copies from the two centuries under consideration have been compared and it was found that they are substantially the same! The main teaching of the Gospel, that Jesus died for our sins and rose again on the third day is still there in all Gospels whatever century the copies are from."

Where does *ayah* 5:47 say that the Christian creed is correct or that the Four Gospels are the Injil of Prophet `Esa (Jesus), peace be on him? Where does *ayah* 5:47 command the People of the Book to believe in the current Bible? This is not the topic of the *ayah*.

Can 'Creed' be Confused with 'Law'?

Has the questioner noticed the word in the *ayah*, '**Wal-Ya`hkum**,' which means, 'Let [them] judge'? '*Hukm*,' is not, creed; '*Hukm*,' is judgment, i.e., it pertains to the Law. This *ayah* has nothing to do with the Christian creed or with Christians, who worship Jesus, because Allah already declared in the Quran that their creed is false, {*Surely, disbelievers are those who said: "Allâh is the third of the three* (in a Trinity)." *But there is no Ilâh* (god) (none who has the right to be worshipped) *but One Ilâh* (God — Allâh).} (5:73)

Also, Allah said, {*Surely, in disbelief are they who say that Allâh is the Messiah, son of Maryam* (Mary). *Say* (O, Muhammad): *"Who then has the least power against Allâh, if He were to destroy the Messiah, son of Maryam* (Mary), *his mother, and all those who are on the earth together?" And to Allâh belongs the dominion of the heavens and the earth, and all that is between them. He creates what He wills. And Allâh is Able to do all things.}* (5:17)

Produce the Injil and we shall honor it, no doubt. Many Christians and even some Muslims think that the Four Gospels that Christians have today comprise the Injil. It is a fact that the current Four Gospels the Christians have are 'popularly' thought to be written by Mark, Luke, Matthew and John. These Gospels are by means the Injil. *Ayah* 5:47 does not refer to these Gospels, which were all written after Jesus was ascended to heaven, alive and well. The Injil is a divinely revealed book sent down **to** Jesus, before he was ascended to heaven.

Judaism and Christendom do not have a single exact replica of anything found in the Bible, whether the Old Testament or the New Testament. Thousands of the oldest manuscripts of the New Testament are available, but no two are exactly the same. The oldest of these were written generations after Jesus departed this earth, alive. No one knows exactly who wrote the Four Gospels or in which original language or time-frame they were written, who translated them, edited them, or testified to the accuracy of the news found in them. This is a mystery that rivals the mystery of Trinity itself.

The Injil is a revelation that came to Prophet `Esa (Jesus), peace be on him. Thus, where the

56

reference to Injil is found in the Quran and Sunnah, it is made to the original copy of the book that Allah revealed to His Prophet Esa. Christians do not have it.

'*Wal-Ya'hkum,'* in *ayah* 5:47, is a continuation of the *ayah* before it, {*And in their footsteps, We sent 'Îsâ* (Jesus), *son of Maryam* (Mary), *confirming the Taurât* (Torah) *that had come before him, and We gave him the Injeel* (Gospel), *in which was guidance and light and confirmation of the Taurât* (Torah) *that had come before it, a guidance and an admonition for al-Muttaqûn* (the pious). *Let the people of the Injeel* (Gospel) *judge by what Allâh has revealed therein. And whosoever does not judge by what Allâh has revealed* (then) *such* (people) *are the Fâsiqûn* [the rebellious] *to Allâh.*} (5:46)

The two *ayat* indicate that Allah revealed the Injil to Prophet `Esa, also sent with confirmation of the Torah such as affirming the law of stoning the adulterers (which Islam upheld, but the Jews and Christians suspended and abandoned).

In the Injil there was guidance for the Children of Israel who were commanded to abide by it. Jesus, as he said in the New Testament, was only sent to the Children of Israel (*Matthew* 15:24).

Thus, the *ayat* under discussion are not divided from what's before or after them. Allah says that He sent Jesus to the Children of Israel and revealed to him the Injil, saying to them, 'Let the people to whom the Injil was sent rule (judge; *wal-Ya'hkum*) by the Injil.' This commandment was given to the people who received the original Injil ordering them to abide by its Law. These *ayat* do not command the Christians to believe in the New Testament; this is a fabrication nowhere to be found in the Quran. *The New Testament is not the Injil.*

The *ayat* before 5:46-47 give the same commandment to the Children of Israel with regards to the Torah: {*Verily, We did send down the Taurât (Torah) [to Mûsâ (Moses)], therein was guidance and light, by which the Prophets, who submitted themselves to Allâh's Will, judged for the Jews. And the rabbis and the priests* [too judged for the Jews by the Taurât (Torah) after those Prophets], *for to them was entrusted the protection of Allâh's Book, and they were witnesses thereto. Therefore fear not men but fear Me* (O, Jews) *and sell not My Verses for a miserable price. And whosoever does not judge by what Allâh has revealed, such are the Kâfirûn* (i.e. disbelievers). *And We ordained therein for them: Life for life, eye for eye, nose for nose, ear for ear, tooth for tooth, and wounds equal for equal. But if anyone remits the retaliation by way of charity, it shall be for him an expiation. And whosoever does not judge by that which Allâh has revealed, such are the Dhâlimûn* (polytheists and wrongdoers).}

Again, Allah states here that He sent down the Torah to the Children of Israel and ordered them to, 'Let those who received the Torah act on its law.' This is the instruction that came to them in the book that Allah revealed to them. This instruction is not about the future, it is not about the present; it was specifically said to those who received the original Torah. Obviously, it was said **to them** in the present tense, because the Children of Israel were supposed to rule by the book not in the past, not in the future, but as soon as they received it and as long as it remained valid.

The instruction in these *ayat* is about abiding by the Law. A hint: 'Life for life,' is a law to act upon, it is not a creed. The Law of the Torah mostly remained valid until the Quran was revealed.

I said, *the Torah*, not, the Old Testament, because the Torah does not exist anymore in its original form. No one knows who wrote the numerous books found in the Old Testament. The five books of Moses were not written by Moses. Moses could not have possibly reported what age he was when he **died**, *"And Moses was an hundred and twenty years old when he **died**: his eye was not dim, nor his natural force abated"* (**Deuteronomy** 34:7).

The *ayat* under discussion continue, because they are still on the same topic, i.e., ruling by what Allah has revealed, {*And We have sent down to you* (O, Muhammad) *the Book* (this Qur'ân) *in truth, confirming the Scripture that came before it and Mohayminan* (trustworthy in highness and a witness) *over it* (old Scriptures). *So judge among them by what Allâh has revealed, and follow not their vain desires, diverging away from the truth that has come to you. To each among you, We have prescribed a law and a clear way. If Allâh had willed, He would have made you one nation, but that* (He) *may test you in what*

He has given you; so compete in good deeds. The return of you (all) *is to Allâh; then He will inform you about that in which you used to differ. And so judge* (you O, Muhammad) *among them by what Allâh has revealed and follow not their vain desires, but beware of them lest they turn you* (O, Muhammad) *far away from some of that which Allâh has sent down to you. And if they turn away, then know that Allâh's Will is to punish them for some sins of theirs. And truly, most of men are Fâsiqûn* (rebellious and disobedient to Allâh).}

Thus, the *ayat* continue, by saying, "We sent Muhammad to you, O, Humankind, and revealed to him a book that **overrules** all the previous books that We revealed before it. So, judge by Our revelation to Muhammad, as the People of the Two Books were ordered to judge by their respective Books while their books were still valid and not corrupted."

Chapter Eight: Christians vs. the Law of Moses

If the questioner believes in what he says, then *ayah* 5:47 would be ordering him and all those who claim to be Christian to rule by the Law of Moses, including life for life, tooth for tooth, stoning for the adulterer, and circumcision. Is he and are Christians willing to do that?

The questioner also forgot to mention the next *ayat* to 5:47 which declare that the law of previous prophets was overruled by the sending of the Quran and Sunnah. This emphasizes the fact that the previous *ayat* were addressed to the nations that received the Torah and the Injil, **before the sending of Muhammad**, peace be on him. Will the questioner then, if he believes in what he says, rule by the Quran and Sunnah?

Therefore, even if humankind now has access to the original copies of the Torah and the Injil, they are still required to rule by the Quran and its Law, {**Say** (O, Muhammad) *"O people of the Scripture* (Jews and Christians)*! You have nothing* (as regards guidance) *until you act according to the Taurât* (Torah), *the Injeel* (Gospel), *and what has* (now) *been sent down to you from your Lord* (the Qur'ân)." *Verily, that which has been sent down to you* (O, Muhammad) *from your Lord increases in most of* *them* (their) ***obstinate rebellion and disbelief. So be not sorrowful over the people who disbelieve.}*** (5:68)

Allah ordered the Children of Israel, the only recipients of the Torah and the Injil, to abide by their law; He warned them against not ruling by what He has revealed.

Following is the story behind the revelation of these *ayat*. Here is a segment from a book titled, ***Holy wars; Crusades; Jihad,*** "The New Testament testifies to the fact that stoning the adulterer was the Law of Prophet Moses, peace be on him, '*4. They say unto him, Master, this woman was taken in adultery, in the very act. 5. Now Moses in the law commanded us, that such should be stoned: but what sayest thou?*' (***John*** 8:4-5) Islam only upheld this divine law. Abdullah ibn `Umar said, 'The Jews came to Allah's Prophet and told him that a man and a woman from amongst them had committed adultery. Allah's Prophet said to them, ***'What do you find in the Torah about the legal punishment of ar-Rajm*** (stoning)?' They replied, '(But) we announce their crime and lash them.' `Abdullah bin Salam (who used be a Jewish Rabi` before he became Muslim) said, 'You are telling a lie; Torah contains the order of stoning.' They brought and opened the Torah and one of them solaced his hand on the verse of stoning and read the verses preceding and following it. `Abdullah bin Salam said to him, 'Lift your hand.' When he lifted his hand, the verse of stoning was written there. They said, 'Muhammad has told the truth; the Torah has the verse of stoning.' The Prophet then gave the order that both of them should be stoned to death.' (*Sahih Al-Bukhari* 3363, and, *Sahih Muslim* 3211)." (*Holy wars; Crusades; Jihad*, Jalal Abualrub, Pg., 46-47, 2nd footnote)

By simply referring to *ayah* 5:43, the context of the *ayat* under discussion becomes clear in that it is about law not about creed, {*But how do they come to you for decision while they have the Taurât* (Torah), *in which is the* (plain) *Decision of Allâh; yet even after that, they turn away. For they are not* (really) *believers.*} (5:43)

Muslims were also commanded, in the present tense, to abide by the revelation that came to Muhammad, peace be on him, and were warned against defying its law. After the Quran was revealed, People of the Scriptures were commanded to abide by Quran's Law. This is the meaning of, '*Muhaimin.*' They have in their books the description of Muhammad, peace be on him, and part of their law conforms to the Quran. If People of the Scriptures truly rule by their books, they will believe in the sending of Prophet Muhammad, peace be on him, which was mentioned in their books. And then, if they are sincere, they will act on the Quran and its Law, part of which they already have in their books.

The *ayat* **do not** say that Christians should believe in the New Testament or Trinity, {*O, people of the Scripture* (Christians)*! Do not exceed the limits in your religion, nor say of Allâh aught but the truth. The Messiah 'Îsâ* (Jesus), *son of Maryam* (Mary)*, was* (no more than) *a Messenger of Allâh and His Word,*

("Be!" — and he was) *which He bestowed on Maryam* (Mary) *and a spirit* (Rûh) *created by Him; so believe in Allâh and His Messengers. Say not: "Three* (trinity)*!" Cease!* (It is) *better for you. For Allâh is* (the only) *One Ilâh* (God), *glory is to Him* (Far Exalted is He) *above having a son. To Him belong all that is in the heavens and all that is in the earth. And Allâh is All-Sufficient as a Disposer of affairs.*} (4:171)

Inventing Religion in Progress

The statement the questioner came with next is astounding, to say the least, "The danger one faces when confronted with extreme or complicated ideas, is, 'to throw the baby out with the bath-water,' this means to reject everything about a matter, even the true and the good. Here is what C.S. Lewis, professor of Medieval and Renaissance literature at Cambridge University has to say about such an attitude: 'If Christianity was something we were making up, of course we could make it easier. But it is not. We cannot compete, in simplicity, with people who are inventing religions. How could we? We are dealing with Fact. Of course anyone can be simple if he has no facts to bother about.' ('Mere Christianity', Macmillan Company, New York, 1943, page 145)"

'Inventing Religion'? From beginning to end, the Old Testament speaks of the One and Only Lord in simple terms, "*Look unto me, and be ye saved, all the*

ends of the earth: for I am God, and there is none else."
(*Isaiah* 45:22). The Old Testament never said God is
three or that He had or will have a son. The Old
Testament never said that this supposed son will die
on the cross to atone for mankind for their sins.

The New Testament also speaks of the One and
Only God, *"For it is written, Thou shalt worship the Lord
thy God, and him only shalt thou serve"* (*Luke* 4:8). Only,
means, only, not three.

The current Christian creed was never before
preached by any prophet whom Allah sent. The
words and concepts the Christians use to justify their
creed are not from their holy book, but are their own
words. If the people the questioner quotes here were
truthful, they would not have needed their own
words, which are complex and utterly confusing, to
justify what they claim the Bible says. They would
have come up with biblical evidence that does not
need to be explained, but instead is self-explanatory.

Moses did not invent a religion, Christians,
did. Moses never knew God as Christians know Him.
Abraham never said what Christians say; Jacob never
said what Christians say. Jesus never spoke of the
complex ideas Christians came up with. The New
Testament does not have complex words like the
words Christians came up with.

Who is inventing religion? Are they those who
abide by the clear proof in the Old Testament, the
New Testament and the Quran that God is One, and
only One? Or, are they the inventors of Trinity who

came up with a creed never heard of before in any revealed book or by the words of any sent prophet?

Is God a Community?

The questioner then makes another astounding statement, "The concept of God being a unique community within Himself stands in opposite to the Muslim concept of Allah being one in the strict numerical sense of the word."

A 'unique community by Himself'! To begin with, the God of the Old Testament made it clear He is One in the strict numerical sense of the word, "*Thou shalt have no other gods before me.*" (*Exodus* 20:3). There is not a single statement in the Old Testament that even hints to Trinity.

No prophet, including Jesus, ever contradicted this fact, "*And when he was gone forth into the way, there came one running, and kneeled to him, and asked him, Good Master, what shall I do that I may inherit eternal life? And Jesus said unto him, Why callest thou me good? there is none good but one, that is, God*" (*Mark* 10:17-18).

This proves that "I AM" was inserted in the New Testament and falsely ascribed to Jesus. In *Mark* 10:17-18, Jesus says that God is **but one**; he did not say God is but three in one, and certainly did not say, "YUP, I AM GOOD."

It has been installed in the conscience of humankind since the time of Adam that God is One.

Yet, according to Christians, God did not inform His creation about His being a community of three, until decades after Jesus was ascended to heaven. Countless thousands of years have passed since Adam, then the series of prophets who came after him, during which God sent countless prophets and revealed to them countless divine books and revelations. Yet, not a single one of them knew anything about the Christian community of gods.

Consequently, if we were to believe Christians, God deceived all of humankind before suddenly deciding to inform them that He is a community of gods. This decision did not come in the Old Testament, the New Testament, or the Quran. Not even Saul (Paul) propagated three gods. Rather, a community of 4th century elders developed, which means, invented a new religion without authority from God or a revealed book to guide them.

Eternal Essence of God

The questioner continues, "This Muslim understanding raises three questions: **i) 'How could Allah have been self sufficient and loving before the creation of angels and of the earth?'**"

Allah being Self-sufficient responds effectively to this question and its implication. Allah is *As-Samad*, the Self-Sufficient, in that He does not need creation, but creation stands in need of Him. In other words, Allah does not need to fulfill His attributes or satisfy a need to love or hate anyone. The very word 'need' contradicts Allah's perfect essence.

Needs, wants and the eagerness to be fulfilled are all a part of creation itself. After Allah created creation and they started receiving His care, love and generosity, His essence did not change as compared to before He created. He did not become fulfilled now that He created and started loving the creation. This is because Allah does not need to love; creation needs Allah to love them.

Christians must think of Allah in what is suitable to His Majesty, not according to their limited life and comprehension. Creation cannot imagine what Allah should be like, and cannot consider His essence anything similar to their essence.

Love Only Comes in Threes

Next, the questioner continues to lower Allah to the level of humans, who need to love and be loved, by saying, "Since true love is always giving and Allah according to Islam is a lone God, according to logic there must have been a time where he was incomplete, where he could not have had the attribute of love? Furthermore, love between two is reciprocal ('I love you and therefore you love me back in return'). It is 'inferior' to shared love between three, as found in the Trinity, being love's fullest expression. (See Richard St Victor in his six books on Trinity)"

First, the notion of true love being always giving is false. Even in human concepts, love can be one sided and can lead its people to horrific crimes in the name of love. Love could be giving, but only in a limited sense as one cannot keep loving, i.e., giving, their entire life, because obviously they have a life to live and numerous other emotions to fulfill.

The questioner is defining the essence of Allah based on the essence of humans and their deficient existence and shortcomings. The very notion that Allah will not be fulfilled and will feel that He is alone mean that the questioner is equating the Creator with creation when it is He Who created these feelings and needs in them.

Having three gods, who need each other to fulfill their attributes, means that each one of them is deficient, by definition. If they need each other to escape a sense of loneliness and un-fulfillment, then none of them is perfect in their essence and none of them can cope with the fullness of their attributes. Allah says in the Quran, {*They made not a just estimate of Allâh such as is due to Him. And on the Day of Resurrection the whole of the earth will be grasped by His Hand and the heavens will be rolled up in His Right Hand. Glorified be He, and High be He above all that they associate as partners with Him!*} (39:67).

The 99 Names of Allah, Again

The questioner continues with his notion of equating Allah with creation, by saying that "Numerous other eternal attributes of Allah which are expressed in his 99 beautiful names can also be used to point towards a contradiction within Allah's being. For him to be the eternal 'El-Hadi', 'the Guide' or, 'El Ghafer,' 'the Forgiver', there must be a created subject where He can be guiding and forgiving. However, according to both the Quran and the Bible, God has always been and always will be perfect, independent from His creation."

If, as the questioner admits, the Quran and the Bible state that Allah is perfect, independent from His creation, then by definition, He does not need them to be fulfilled, to begin with. The questioner defeats his own reasoning by asserting that the Bible and the Quran say that Allah is One, thus admitting that Trinity is not in the Bible, and obviously, not in the Quran.

Christian concept of God contrasts sharply to the Islamic concept of Allah. Allah said in the Quran, {*O, Mankind! It is you who stand in need of Allâh. But Allâh is Rich* (Free of all needs), *Worthy of all praise.*} (35:15)

Therefore, the fact that Allah is *Al-Hadi*, the One Who guides, has two parts. It is an eternal attribute of Allah that is always perfect, i.e., just like

Him, does not stand in need of creation to guide them so as to be fulfilled. The second part is that where there is creation in need of guidance, then, Allah will guide them because he is *Al-Hadi*.

Even if one discusses human beings, one will find the reasoning of the questioner deficient. Those whose nature is generous, kind, and easy going, or are miserly, harsh and difficult, have these qualities or shortcomings installed within them. Then, when they are confronted by the opportunity to be generous, kind and easy going, or the opposite of these traits, their nature will become manifest in the action they will then take. Both before and after they act on their nature, they will still have these traits or shortcomings within them installed in their nature and essence of existence.

Just because a generous person cannot keep giving throughout their entire life, does not mean they are not generous by nature. Nature is the essence, while acting on nature is the consequence or the effect of one's nature; they are not one and the same. What about the Creator of all things, why would He need to prove Himself to His creation, if He is free from defects that is?

Chapter Nine: Does God Need Creation?

It is an obvious contradiction to state that Allah is independent from creation yet stands in need of them to be fulfilled. For instance, among Allah's names is, '*Al-Awwal*,' meaning, 'The First.' If we use the logic of the questioner, then if Allah is the First yet needed creation from the beginning to fulfil His attribute 'the Creator,' then He will not be the First. This is because there will always be another first with Him, meaning a creation He needed to fulfil His attributes through them.

The questioner might say here that the Son and the Holy Ghost where with God from eternity. This will not answer his question, because the Son and the Holy Ghost are already eternally guided, so we are told. Therefore, God would still need creation who existed with Him from eternity, so He can grant them guidance, food, drink, a physical body, life, happiness, cure for illness, and so forth.

In addition, the Old Testament and the Quran have not indicated in the slightest way that God is three; this information is news to these books and to all the prophets whom God sent to guide their respective nations. If we again use the questioner's logic here, then, as agreed, God is the One Who guides. Yet, He did not inform His own prophets, let alone the rest of creation, that He is actually three in one and one in three. Therefore, this attribute of His was not fulfilled from eternity, but was deficient from eternity, until Trinity suddenly appeared in the 4th century.

God was before creation and this is the essence of His being Eternal. Therefore, according to the questioner's logic, these attributes of God found in the Old Testament and the New Testament were not fulfilled from eternity:

First: *"I, the Lord your God, am a jealous God, punishing the children for the sin of the fathers"* (*Exodus* 20:5). Did God develop this jealousy of sin and Polytheism after He created creation, or was it present in Him from eternity, and if so, who was there to sin to arouse God's jealousy?

According to Christians, God was three in one from eternity. Was jealousy against sin shared between them, against each other, or was it suppressed in all of them, because there was no creation yet to fulfill this attribute?

In addition, *Exodus* 20:5 claims that God punishes the innocent for the sins of the guilty? In contrast, Islam says that Allah does not punish the children for the mistakes of their fathers, {*Whoever goes right, then he goes right only for the benefit of his ownself. And whoever goes astray, then, he goes astray to his own loss. No one laden with burdens can bear another's burden. And We never punish until We have sent a Messenger* (to give warning).} (17:15)

73

The false claim that God punishes the innocent for the crimes of the guilty is consistent with the invented creed of Original Sin. This rejected false claim ascribes injustice to Allah, and it is not less wicked than the claim that God cannot accept direct repentance from His slaves without punishing someone else for their sins, {*And when My slaves ask you* (O, Muhammad) *concerning Me, then* (answer them), *I am indeed near* (to them by My Knowledge). *I respond to the invocations of the supplicant when he calls on Me* (without any mediator or intercessor). *So let them obey Me and believe in Me, so that they may be led aright.*} (2:186).

Second: "*He guides the humble in what is right and teaches them his way*" (**Psalms** 25:9).

Thus, according to the Old Testament, God is *Al-Hadi*, He Who guides. If God were *Al-Hadi* from eternity, whom was He guiding and showing them the way? Or, did He develop this attribute after creation? Or, was He guiding and showing the way to the Holy Ghost and the Son from eternity, until He created 'humble' creation that needed to be guided by Him?

Third: "*If anyone chooses to do God's will, he will find out whether my teaching comes from God or whether I speak on my own*" (**John** 7:17).

Christians claim that Jesus is God, eternal. Did he fulfill his need to teach and guide creation and to speak to them from eternity, or were these attributes of his unfulfilled and untested? Or, did Jesus guide

74

God and the Holy Ghost, or suppress this need until creation came and then he joined them temporarily?

(*John* 7:17) clearly states that what Jesus taught came from God, not from his own self. Therefore, Jesus is not God, since he stated that he received knowledge from God not from himself. In addition, this proves that Jesus was a Prophet from God, since his mission was to convey God's will.

Fourth: "*And the Lord ... proclaimed, The Lord, The Lord God, merciful and gracious, long-suffering, and abundant in goodness and truth*" (*Exodus* 34:6).

Thus, according to the Old Testament, God is merciful, gracious, patient, and possessor of all goodness and truth, the equivalent of Allah's Islamic names, '*Ar-Ra`heem; Ash-Shakur; As-Sabur; Al-`Haqq.*' How were these attributes tested, if they existed from eternity before there were any to grant mercy to, to be patient with their errors, to thank them for doing good, to grant them abundance in righteousness?

According to the questioner's logic, these attributes were not fulfilled; they were dormant, idle, alone, until there was creation to receive these benefits. The presence of two more gods did not help fulfill these traits, which are not suitable for the Holy Ghost or the Son since according to Christians, they are gods, perfect beings who stand in no need of guidance, they do not err, they do not need to thank God since they are Him, and they are eternally righteous.

The questioner's logic thus applies to his holy books, unless he claims that creation is also eternal, meaning, from the beginning there were creations that erred and God was jealous of their errors, creations He guided and loved. Whatever answers the questioner may come up with to these questions, will expose the deficient logic Christians have about God and the Quran.

As for the questioner's argument that God was 'loved' within the Trinity, so this attribute of His was fulfilled, it is rejected by his own Bible, which claims two Gods not three, *"In the beginning was the Word, and the Word was with God, and the Word was God"* *(John* 1:1). What happened to the Holy Ghost here? *John* 1:1 seems to have forgotten that the Holy Ghost was also in the beginning and was also God, according to Christian creed.

The More Gods the Better the Love Shared Between Them

Did God also love mankind, us, from eternity "To think that God gave up a perfect relationship for a time shows how great his love towards us is!"?

If yes, then creation is eternal. If no, then God's love *for creation*, 'us,' developed as much in the same way as Trinity was developed centuries after Jesus departed this earth. Also, if being three-in-one and one-in-three makes better love between the gods than being just one, then why not four gods, or five hundred gods? Why only three? The more gods, the better the love shared between them! Then the mystery will be far more substantial. We seek refuge with Allah from all this which belittles Him and degrades His perfect essence.

Number of Allah's Names

Allah has more than 99 Names, {*And* (all) *the Most Beautiful Names belong to Allâh, so call on Him by them, and leave the company of those who belie or deny* (or utter impious speech against) *His Names. They will be requited for what they used to do.*} (7:180)

The questioner is confused. First, he belittles the role of the Prophet's Sunnah by claiming that it is of a lesser value to the Quran. Yet, he is stuck on the notion of a list of Allah's 99 names. However, neither the number 99, nor a specific list of the 99 names can be found in the Quran to begin with.

The authentic Sunnah mentions the number 99. A *hadeeth* states, "*Allah has ninety-nine Names, one hundred minus one; whoever believes in their meanings and acts accordingly, will enter Paradise*" (*Sahih Al-Bukhari*, hadeeth no. 6410).

The narration that lists the 99 names is not established; the chain of narration reporting the list is weak (*Dha`eef At-Trimidhi*, Al-Albani, *hadeeth* no. 3507). The narrator who reported this list is not a reliable narrator as many scholars attested, including At-Tirmidhi, Ibn 'Hazm, Ibn Kathir, As-Suyuti, Al-Wadi'i, and so forth.

Does God Feel Lonely?

Aloneness, boredom, dependence, need, un-fulfilment are all but some of Allah's creation. They do not bind Him, they are subservient to Him. Humankind does not and should not be allowed to bind Allah by their inferior human logic, {*Allâh stands not in need of any of the 'Âlamîn* (all that exists)} (3:97).

The questioner continues with a stunning question, "'**Is Allah selfish?**' Since love is described as having '... no envy ... no high opinion of itself ... no pride ... no thought for itself ... (1 Cor 13: 4-5) some people like sceptic John Stuart Mill, Mark Twain or Pablo Picasso have come to the conclusion that God is utterly selfish. They say that by asking us to worship nobody else but God, he himself commits the sin of seeking glory for himself only for which he condemns man. While many Muslims would say that Allah, the creator can be selfish if he wants, Bible believing Christians find the answer to this apparent contradiction in the Trinitarian nature of God. He shares his glory among himself."

This is a terrible description of the Creator of all things especially coming from some of the most immoral western men who led a life of disobedience to God, their Creator. To state that Allah commits a sin, because He only allows worship of Himself alone, is an awful statement of disbelief, as well as, a ridiculous, absurd notion.

Why would Allah allow worship of others besides Him, when He Alone created and sustained all that exists, {*Say* (O, Muhammad)*: "Who is the Lord of the heavens and the earth?" Say: "(It is) Allâh." Say: "Have you then taken* (for worship) *Auliyâ'* (protectors) *other than Him, such as have no power either for benefit or for harm to themselves?" Say: "Is the blind equal to the one who sees? Or darkness equal to light?"*} (13:16)

God does not seek glory; He owns it, {*Whosoever desires honor, power and glory then to Allâh belong all honor, power and glory*} (35:10). Therefore, those who seek honor, power and glory can only attain these qualities from Allah, and only by obeying and worshipping Him Alone. In addition, how can Allah, the Exalted, be envious of His own creation, when they are nothing without Him, {*But Allâh is Rich* (Free of all needs), *and you* (humankind) *are poor*} (47:38)?

According to the logic of the questioner and the three immoral men he quoted, it is not only the Quran, but also the Old Testament and the New Testament that call to the worship of a selfish envious God, since all three books emphasize only one God.

Love has a different meaning with regards to the Islamic religion pertaining to God. The questioner seems to use concepts that limit the creation and apply them to the Creator. For instance, being 'Selfish,' contradicts the nature of Allah the Most Generous, {*O, Man! What has made you careless about your Lord, the Most Generous? Who created you, fashioned you perfectly, and gave you due proportion.*} (82:6-7)

By claiming that God is selfish in that He demands He alone is worshipped, the questioner contradicts the very essence of the Old Testament. Moses said that God is one Lord, described as being *jealous* and demanding that He Alone is worshipped, *"Thou shalt not bow down thyself to them, nor serve them: for I the Lord thy God am a jealous God"* (***Exodus*** 20:5).

In addition, if we believe the questioner's logic, then Jesus must have called to an envious, selfish God when he said, *"Get thee behind me, Satan: for it is written, Thou shalt worship the Lord thy God, and him only shalt thou serve"* (***Luke*** 4:8). Contemplate how pure the monotheism Jesus called to, and how deluded from the truth are those who ascribe partners to Allah. Further, in no language does '*him only*' mean '*the three of them only.*'

The same notion the questioner accuses God of, being selfish because He demands He alone is worshipped, is said about a company of three who demand that they 'alone' be worshipped. Three can also be selfish and envious, why restrict the number of gods to three? The more gods to worship, the less selfish and envious they become, if we were to adopt the questioner's logic that is.

The same evil description, selfish, the questioner uses to describe Allah with, applies to the Christian God as well, since Christians insist they worship only one God. If Christians truly believe that God is one, and since the Bible states that God demands that He alone is worshipped (**Luke** 4:8), then the false description of being selfish applies to Him, as well. Unless, of course, Christians admit the truth, that is, they worship multiple gods not one. Allah is praised from such clear disbelief in Him.

Humankind is mostly unjust. Allah Alone created them, Allah Alone sustains them, Allah Alone owns their life and death, Allah Alone gives them food and drink. Therefore, Allah, Alone, deserves to be worshipped, without partners. However, most humankind is being ungrateful to Allah, {*They recognize the Grace of Allâh, yet they deny it* (by worshipping others besides Allâh) *and most of them are disbelievers*} (16:83).

Why would humankind eat Allah's food, breath His air yet thank for these bounties those who did not create them, but are themselves created, {*All praises and thanks be to Allâh, Who* (Alone) *created the heavens and the earth, and originated the darkness and the light; yet those who disbelieve hold others as equal with their Lord. He it is Who has created you from clay, and then has decreed a* (stated) *term* (for you to die). *And there is with Him another determined term* (for you to be resurrected), *yet you*

81

doubt (in the Resurrection). *And He is Allâh* (to be worshipped Alone) *in the heavens and on the earth; He knows what you conceal and what you reveal, and He knows what you earn* (good or bad).} (6:1-3)

Pertaining to the invented Christian notion of God vs. Love, it seems that God's love did not extend to the countless humans who lived and died unaware of Jesus' sacrifice and his being divine, or about the true religion as Christians profess it. Why did God wait all this time before letting humankind in on the secret? Why did He not extend His Love to those who came before Jesus by letting Jesus die on the cross before Adam was created, or at least soon after Adam was created and during his lifetime, so they can benefit from his sacrifice and acknowledge it? Why doesn't God, as Christians describe Him, love those who do not believe He has a son or that Jesus died for their sin? How little people think of Allah.

Next, the questioner continues his campaign of describing Allah with shortcomings and being deficient, to justify Trinity, "'**Is Allah limited?'** Of course that can not be, but he who thinks of God as an absolute unity where there is no room for multiplicity at all, is forced to believe in a god who does not know himself. Self-knowledge demands a distinction, a multiplicity, between knower and known. Self-consciousness, the recognition of a creature by itself as a 'self' can only exist in contrast with an 'other', a something which is not the self. Only a Trinitarian concept of God allows for such a vital distinction."

The questioner seems to continue the theme that God needs fulfilment of His attributes; that Allah needs to be known by others, or at least by His multiple self, for Him to earn self-knowledge.

According to the questioner's logic, and to solve this shortcoming in God it seems, the Triune Council shared knowledge about God between themselves and thus God-ness was somehow fulfilled. However, since the questioner states that God is one, not three gods, then, his logic does not solve the shortcoming, because He is still a lone God in need of discovering Himself through multiplicity, so the questioner says. If the questioner admits that Christians worship multiple Gods, he would be contradicting his own statement of faith, "It has to be stated emphatically that Christians do not worship three gods but one God."

If Christians believe that God is one, then the invented notion of God not knowing Himself applies. Yet, God has been creating for countless billions of years. He already has had audience to know and recognize Him. God has had the opportunity to know Himself through creation, and therefore, He is no longer alone or unaware of Himself, if we believe the questioner's logic that is. The questioner would not have resorted to such nonsense had he admitted that Trinity is an invented religion that demeans God and belittles Him to no end. We seek refuge with Allah, Creator of all things, from this disbelief. This is reinventing God in process.

Chapter Ten: Is Allah Aware of Himself?

Allah said, in the Quran, that He revealed the Quran with His knowledge, {*But Allâh bears witness to that which He has sent down* (the Qur'ân) *unto you* (O, Muhammad); *He has sent it down with His Knowledge, and the angels bear witness. And Allâh is All-Sufficient as a Witness.*} (4:166)

Therefore, Allah 'knew' that He is *Al-Hadi* when He spoke with the Quran *before* creating creation. This is the proof: Imam Muslim (4797) collected a *hadeeth* in which Allah's Prophet stated that fifty thousand years before creating the heavens and earth, Allah wrote the destiny of all creation.

Therefore, the fact that in the Quran, Allah announced some of His attributes to His creation is proof of self-knowledge, since before He created creation, as the *hadeeth* above states, Allah had everything that will happen to creation recorded and scribed. This includes listing His names and attributes and the benefit humankind will gain from His names and attributes.

Do Muslims Worship Two Gods?

The questioner invents a strange notion, next, then ascribes it to Islam, "**Are there two Eternal Ones in Islam?'** According to orthodox Islam the Quran is the uncreated, eternal word of God which has always existed in heaven, written in the form of tablets. The Mu'tazilites recognized that this would lead to the existence of two Eternal Ones and were therefore saying that the Quran was not everlasting. However, they are considered, Non Muslim heretics."

We had agreed with the questioner to only discuss the true resources of Islam not what Islamic sects say. However, I will still answer his question.

First, it is not true that the *Mu`tazilah* are considered non-Muslims. The questioner is confused. The *Mu'tazilah* are considered a deviant sect, yet, their deviation is not of the type that takes one out of the fold of Islam. 'Deviant,' does not necessarily mean 'disbeliever.'

Second, the questioner is also confused between what is an attribute of Allah and Allah Himself. For instance, Allah's *Kalam*, meaning, Speech, is among His attributes, eternal; Allah speaks with what He will whenever He will. His speech does not only include the Quran, but the original Torah, Zabur and Injil are also part of Allah's speech.

The result of Allah's eternal attribute, *Kalam*, is that the Torah, the Injil and the Quran proceeded from Him, from His Quality of *Kalam*. Allah's attribute of *Kalam* is therefore not created, because Allah is not created and His attributes are not created. They are a part of His perfect existence.

The *Mu'tazilah* logic did not come from the Quran, but from silly philosophy. They are similar to the questioner and many other Christians in that they imagine with their limited mind how Allah should be like, deciding for Him what attributes He can or cannot have. *Mu`tazilah* did not consider the Quran as the literal word of Allah, but as a creation. However, all creation dies, but the Quran is still alive and well fourteen centuries after it was revealed.

Mu'tazilah thought that if they agree -with Allah that is- that Allah speaks, then, His *Kalam* becomes a separate eternal entity different from Him. Consequently, *Mu'tazilah* first feared multiplicity, to use the questioner's own words, then based on this imaginary fear, they denied Allah's attribute, *Kalam*, and claimed that the Quran is created.

Is Human Speech a Separate Entity?

Simply put: even the questioner will not say that his speech is a different entity than he is. The questioner has many other qualities shared by other humans: they move, act, breathe and have kindness, generosity, courage, life, etc. Who would say that all these are separate entities from men and women, and as such, are separate creations? Who would say that one's words are a separate entity from the person who spoke them?

Mu`tazilah failed, just like the questioner, to fully understand the topic. Allah's attributes are His qualities; they are a consequence of His perfect existence and perfect essence. Thus Allah is Able to speak: the Quran is His words, the Quran is not Allah Himself; it cannot act independently, create, or have a life of its own, because it is an attribute, a quality, not a person or a god.

When the questioner repeated *Mu'tazilah* concepts, he exposed their ignorance such as the invented notion of the tablets being eternal, which no Muslim scholar says. The questioner also invented a theme that even *Mu'tazilah* did not invent: *Mu'tazilah* do not use the argument that, "the uncreated, eternal word of God which has always existed in heaven, written in the form of tablets."

Mu'tazilah do not believe that heaven always existed. To the contrary, *Mu'tazilah* came up with an absurd notion that Paradise (heaven) has not been created yet; otherwise, it would be empty, since its residents will only enter it after Resurrection. They forget, for example, that paradise already has residents in it who are not humans.

Eternal Tablets

Tablets did not exist from eternity: Here is part of a book that responds to the slander Pope Benedict XVI made against Prophet Muhammad, peace be on him, "In one of his *hadeeths*, Prophet Muhammad informed mankind about Allah's encompassing Knowledge, when he said, '*Right after Allah created the Pen, He said to it, 'Write!' The Pen said, 'What should I write?' Allah said, 'Write al-Qadar: what happened and what will happen for-ever'*' (*Sahih at-Tirmidhi* 2155)" (*50 Righteous and Humane Concepts Brought by Muhammad*, Jalal Abualrub, Pg., 13-14).

Therefore, the tablets did not exist from eternity as the questioner seems to suggest, they went into action after Allah created the Pen, which according to an authentic *hadeeth*, is the first creation, "*The first thing Allah created was the Pen, and He commanded it, and the Pen wrote everything that will happen*" (*Takhreej Kitab As-Sunnah*, Al-Albani, *hadeeth* no. 108). Then, Allah placed the tablets above His Throne (*A`hkam Al-Quran*, Ibn al-`Arabi, 4/420).

The *Mu`tazilah* is indeed a minor cult compared to the vast majority of Muslims who follow the Sunnah way.

Is God a 'Despot'?

The questioner wrote, next, "**Is the teaching of Allah's Oneness responsible for unbalanced Islamic societies?** In the Zabur God says that people will become like the god they worship. (Psalm 135: 15-18) The idea we have of God will influence the society we will create. In Islam God is a lone despot who does what He pleases, consulting no one. Consequently, the Muslim individual is swallowed up in the ummah. We find Islamic, totalitarian states that oppress individual creativity. As a result Muslim states are economically weak, human rights are not followed and freedom of expression is not encouraged. Sadly, in the idolatrous Western Nations of the 21st century where many people worship their idols, we find the other extreme. Community is swallowed up in individualism. The Biblical, Trinitarian description of God, when truly believed and practiced, produces a balanced society where both the individual and the community are equally important. Both are respecting and benefiting each other, leading to peace and progress. (See the late British theologian Colin Gunton addressing the problem of one and many in his book "The One, the Three and the Many", 1993)

First, all believers should reject the questioner's description of the One and Only God worshipped by Adam, Noah, Abraham, Moses, Jesus and

Muhammad, and all prophet's in between, as being a despot, meaning, a tyrant. None of the prophets ever knew God according to the Trinity concept; they all preached the One and Only God...

1. The Old Testament testifies that God is One, *"The Lord our God is one Lord"* (**Deuteronomy** 6:4);
2. The New Testament testifies that God is One, *"The Lord our God is one Lord"* (**Mark** 12:29);
3. The Quran testifies that God is One, {*It is He* (Allâh) *Who is the only Ilâh* (God to be worshipped)} (43:84).

It is astounding, to say the least, to learn how the questioner protests the fact that Allah decides what He will without having to consult anyone. The questioner seems to want Allah to consult Christians on what He should do, how He should be like, and if He is allowed to be Alone or to take partners. This demeaning of Allah (God) is rejected, {*And your Lord creates whatsoever He wills and chooses, no choice have they* (in any matter). *Glorified is Allâh, and exalted above all that they associate* (as partners with Him).} (28:68)

In addition, we agreed with the questioner to debate Islam, not Muslims. Yet, I should state here a fact universally known about Christian societies since Trinity was forced on Christians by a pagan emperor in the fourth century CE.

Here is part of, *50 Righteous and Humane Concepts Brought by Muhammad*, "Trinity was forced into Christianity by Emperor Constantine, who in 325 CE called for the first ecumenical council in church history for the purpose of settling the disputes about the nature of God that arose between various Christian sects.

1. Weeks after the council met, comprised of 318 bishops according to Athanasius as he stated in his letter *Ad Afros*, the doctrine of the Trinity was forced upon Christians as the creed to be followed.

2. Horrific religious persecution followed the decision made by Constantine, essentially a pagan Emperor, to impose an invented creed never preached by Jesus.

3. Even the most fanatical supporters of Trinity cannot scientifically trace modern-day Trinity any farther back than the second Christian century. Even then, it was an alien creed, never propagated by Jesus or by any of his disciples. During that era, Trinity would have competed with other alien theories popular among Christians about the nature of Jesus Christ.

4. True faith in Jesus diminished ever since, until almost disappearing before Islam came." (*50 Righteous and Humane Concepts Brought by Muhammad*, Jalal Abualrub, Pg., 22)

Since then, every Christian state was a model of tyranny, oppression and corruption. Papal States were a classical example of the tyranny of states ruled by Christianity. The questioner seems to forget the extremely bloody conflicts Christian Europe had about and because of Christian religion, and the fact that Europe had to struggle through extremely bloody wars to escape the stranglehold the Christian church had on life, society and science.

Currently, most Christian nations in Eastern Europe, Central and South America, Africa and Asia, are in terrible shape economically, socially, industrially and fiscally, and are being ruled by mostly oppressive, corrupt regimes. Many Muslim countries are better off than most of these poor, backward Christian countries.

What does this say about Trinity then, if we were to use the logic of the questioner? In addition, the multiplicity of deities Christians believe in seems to have a strong relation to the continuing conflict, division, injustice and worship of the individual that Christian societies suffer from.

Popes were and still are emperors described as 'infallible' by the vast majority of Christians. In the past, the papal system of religious government forced everyone to follow their ideas; economy and science suffered under their tyranny. During the Crusades, Christians, who answered the call of the popes to invade the holy land, committed some of the most horrible crimes ever committed by man, killing Jews, Muslims and even Christians who took refuge in churches in Jerusalem.

Yet, through the Crusades, Christians were exposed to the Islamic civilization that Muslims enjoyed under the mercy of Islam and because of Islam. Christians copied the Islamic civilization, which is a direct result of Islam itself and due to the encouragement Islam gives to social harmony, strength and advancement, whether pertaining to military, scientific or economic fields. Christendom copied the Islamic civilization, never thanked Muslims for it then attacked almost every Muslim country on the face of the earth.

What about the Inquisitions; and what happened to Muslims and Jews who lived in Spain prior to Christians occupying it? What about the Americas, which European Christians stole from their true owners and almost led them to virtual extinction? They then forced Christianity upon the survivors, as well as, upon millions of African Muslims who were kidnapped from their homes and villages then shipped to the Americas to become Christians and slaves to Christians.

What about the Philippines, which was mostly Muslim before the Dutch came, but is now mostly Christian after the Dutch and Spaniards left? The Dutch were among the worst, most violent, corrupt, bloody and fanatical of occupiers of other peoples' lands that Europe ever came up with. What about the economic and social misery the Philippines lives in now, even though being extreme Trinitarian fanatics?

What about Christian Africa and the civil wars and misery they live in? Rwanda was not Muslim when Christian on Christian violence led to the death of close to one million people in 1994.

In addition, and just like the Zabur says in that people will become like the god they worship (**Psalms** 135:15-18), Christian societies have become as they have mostly been, rampant with violence and instability. Only a few decades ago, three major Christian European nations, led by two Catholics and an Orthodox, led the world into a disaster of untold proportions by causing the death of at least 120 million human-beings.

"I Am Now as Before a Catholic and Will Always Remain So"

These three Christian men were not Muslim by any means, nor were they quoting the Quran when they did what they did. In fact, Hitler often quoted the Bible against the Jews. It is reported that Hitler once said, "I am now as before a Catholic and will always remain so" (*Adolf Hitler*, John Toland, Pg. 507). He also said, "I believe that I am acting in accordance with the will of the Almighty Creator: by defending myself against the Jew, I am fighting for the work of the Lord" (*Mein Kampf*, Adolf Hitler, Pg. 65).

Stalin was sent by his mother to a covenant school to study Christianity, before he led the Soviet Union and caused the death of one quarter of his own population before WWII.

Mussolini often met with and sought blessing from Catholic Popes, who were at least silent, surely did not object to the extermination of Jews. The Vatican had to apologize to the Jews for its silence, i.e., active participation in some aspects, during and before WWII.

Germany, Italy, France, Poland, Romania, among other nations are not Muslim but Christian nations. They did not quote the Quran when they helped Nazis exterminate the Jews and other nations.

What these individuals and nations did is consistent with what Christian societies, who came before them, did to each other and to Jews and Muslims. Do these bloody wars portray the multiple-personality gods Christians worship? Are Christians torn between a violent despot personality portrayed in the Old Testament and a peaceful triune-personality portrayed in the New Testament?

Which god-personality do Christians emulate? Is it the peaceful personality that calls on them to show the other cheek to those who strike them on their cheek? Or is it the personality of aggression that ordered them to, *"Now go and smite Amalek, and utterly destroy all that they have, and spare them not; but slay both man and woman, infant and suckling, ox and sheep, camel and ass"* (*I Samuel* 15:3)"?

Is not dropping bombs that weigh more than a ton on civilian neighbourhoods in the pretext that a lone terrorist is hiding in that neighbourhood, is not this crime consistent with *I Samuel* 15:3? And why are the self-described religious men and women of the West, especially evangelists, at the forefront of calls to commit armed aggression against Islam and Muslims?

Multiplicity leads to division and chaos, as Allah said, {*Had there been therein* (in the heavens and the earth) *âlihah* (gods) *besides Allâh, then verily, both would have been ruined. Glorified be Allâh, the Lord of the Throne,* (High is He) *above all that* (evil) *they associate with Him!*} (21:22)

Christians have always been confused because of this multiplicity concept. On one hand, they have the Old Testament that reports extreme acts of violence and ascribes them to God, Jesus according to Christians since to them, Jesus revealed the Old Testament. On the other hand, Christians have a new image of God which they created in the New Testament where the same Old Testament warrior God is suddenly portrayed as the prince of peace who came to die for the sins of Christians. The two Gods, the Old Testament God and the New Testament God, are different from each other.

Chapter Eleven: Multiple Gods vs. Cosmic Order

Multiplicity in leadership is always divisive and confusing. Throughout the history of mankind ultimate leadership rested only with one person. More than one leader necessarily leads to disputes, {*No son* (or offspring) *did Allâh beget, nor is there any ilâh* (god) *along with Him.* (If there had been many gods), *then each god would have taken away what he had created, and some would have tried to overcome others! Glorified be Allâh above all that they attribute to Him! All-Knower of the unseen and the seen! Exalted be He over all that they associate as partners to Him!*} (23:91-92)

Muslim leaders and communities the questioner is referring to do have some of the ills he describes, not because of Islam, which by no means calls for such conditions. Rather, it is precisely because many Muslims and their rulers have at least partially ignored ruling by Islamic law, that they have all these troubles and divisions.

The Islamic description of God, <u>when truly believed in and practiced</u>, produces a balanced society where both the individual and the community are equally important. Whenever Islam was strong in the hearts of Muslims, their state was on top of the world, including scientifically and economically.

Both, the Islamic society and the individuals who live in the Islamic society, are respectful of each other, leading them to peace, prosperity and progress. This can only be achieved through fulfilling the unity in creation, which represents unity of the Creator, i.e., Allah is One, and Only One.

Number of Islamic Sects

The questioner next asks questions about Islam and the sect Jalal Abualrub belongs to, "Is it not the case that if a Hadith contradicts the Quran it is not valid? Does that not mean that the Quran is more important than the Hadith. Please tell me exactly what kind of Muslim you are. If you are a Sunni, to what sect do you belong and how do you know it is the right one? According to tradition Muhammad (p.b.u.h.) is quoted as having prophesied that his followers will be divided into 73 sects (Arabic, firac). Every one of them would go to hell, except the one professed by him and his companions. (Mishkat, book 1, ch vi. pt.2). 'The number has, however, far exceeded the Prophets predictions for the sects of Islam, even exceeding in number and variety those of the Christian religion.' (Dictionary of Islam, by T. P. Hughes, Asia Publishing House, London, 1998, p. 567) So is this Hadith authentic even though the prophet predictions have been exceeded?"

Of course I am a Sunni; is not that obvious in my stressing the importance of the Sunnah and the necessity of abiding by the way the Prophet's companions understood and practiced the religion? The Sunni people include the entire Muslim generation of the Prophet, the generation that transferred Islam, Quran and Sunnah, to humankind.

There were no sects during the Prophet's time; there were few individuals who were misguided. The sects developed after the Prophet's death. He, peace be on him, warned against sectarian ways beforehand, because division is a sign of contradicting the Islamic way, and because it is a sin to divide in the religion, *"I have left two matters among you that as long as you hold fast to them you will never go astray: the Book of Allah and my Sunnah"* (*Manzilatu As-Sunnah*, Al-Albani, *hadeeth* no. 13]).

What I, this author, follow is the very generation that learned Islam with its Prophet then transferred it to all Muslims. They are the best people as the Prophet called them, *"The best people are my generation, then the next generation, then the next generation"* (*Bukhari* 2458, and, *Muslim* 4601). They are Muhammad's companions, friends, supporters, relatives and the best believers after Allah's prophets and messengers.

What about the questioner, and what Christian sect does he belong to? Christians are as much divided as Muslims are. Christian sects and cults fill the earth today; they are in endless conflict and dispute with each other, even with regards to the essence of God.

The questioner should first acknowledge the prophecy of the Prophet, who said that Muslims will divide after him, which happened. The *hadeeth* is authentic, of course, *"The Jews and Christians were divided into seventy-one and seventy-two religious sects -respectively, and this nation* (Muslims) *will divide into seventy-three religious sects — all in Hell, except one, and that is the one on which I and my Companions are today"* (*Majmu-`u Al-Fatawa*, Ibn Taimiyyah, 3/345).

In this *hadeeth*, **it is obvious** that the Prophet, peace be on him, acknowledged the fact that sects among Muslims will outnumber Jewish and Christian sects, respectively. In addition, in this *hadeeth*, the Prophet stated that the only sect that will be saved from Hell is the one that follows his way and the way of his companions. This is how Muslims know that the sect that follows the Prophet's companions is the only true sect.

Where is the List?

However, since the questioner did not list the sects that, according to him and the person he quoted, exceed seventy-three, then, how can I explain the truth to him? The problem is that the person he quoted may have come up with sects that he decided

-on his own- as being distinct and different from each other. I sincerely doubt he knows what a sect means according to the *hadeeth*; he is classifying sects according to his own judgment, maybe counting the same sect multiple times unknowing that the name may change, but the essence remains the same.

For example, *Mu'tazilah* sect still exists today, but under various different names, such as the `*Aqlaniyyun*, in reference to those who judge divine text according to the mind, their own mind of course. Thus, the man the questioner quoted may have listed three, four or more sects as being different sects, even though they are just one sect. He may have counted the dozens of sects the Shi`a have divided into, as multiple sects instead of one.

Chapter Twelve: Did Muhammad Contradict the Quran?

Every *hadeeth* said by the Prophet, peace be on him, is valid and authentic. There is not a single *hadeeth* that the Prophet said that contradicts the Quran. The questioner is confused between narrations that are ascribed to the Prophet but have problems in the chains of narration transmitting them, as compared to what has been established as authentic *hadeeths* that the Prophet, peace be on him, said. The same word, *hadeeth*, is used to describe statements that are valid and authentic, and statements that are fabricated or weak.

'Hadeeth' pertains to speech, that is, statements. If a *hadeeth* narration ascribed to the Prophet comes to us through authentic chains of narration that are free from apparent and/or hidden defects, it is accepted, because then we know that the Prophet, peace be on him, said it. If a *hadeeth* ascribed to the Prophet comes to us through weak or rejected chains of narration, then it is not accepted, because the Prophet did not say it; it was falsely ascribed to him. **This is how important the Prophet's *hadeeth* is to Muslims:** an entire community of scholars dedicated their life to preserving the Prophet's *hadeeth*.

102

A sign of weak or rejected *hadeeths*, along with the deficiency in the chains of narration transmitting them, is that the text contradicts the Quran. This is the fabricated or weak *hadeeth*, meaning, statements falsely ascribed to the Prophet, or their narrators made mistakes in what they narrated.

To prove that what the questioner understood is not valid, I should state here that if a *hadeeth* is found to contradict a more established *hadeeth*, not only the Quran, then the *hadeeth* is also rejected. Using his logic, the *hadeeth* of the Prophet must be less important than the *hadeeth* of the Prophet, since if a *hadeeth* of the Prophet is found to contradict another *hadeeth* of the Prophet, then the *hadeeth* of the Prophet is rejected. Better yet, Allah called the Quran itself 'hadeeth', {**Is it such a hadeeth** (this Qur'ân) **that you** (disbelievers) **deny?**} (56:81)

Knowledge of *hadeeth* is about verifying what the Prophet, peace be on him, truly said as compared to what was ascribed to him by mistake and what was falsely ascribed to him.

Next, the questioner writes, "You(r) dictionary quotations above are taken out of context. It is no problem that the word 'Trinity' is not found in the Bible (neither is the Kalima). The doctrine only had to be fully developed in the fourth century by the church as a reaction to false teachers. The church did this based on Bible passages which I sent you above. In the first three centuries there was not need for spelling out explicitly what the Bible said implicitly all along."

Here is the *Kalimah* again, in one Quranic sentence, {*He is Allâh, beside Whom Lâ ilâha illa Huwa* (none has the right to be worshipped but He) *the All-Knower of the unseen and the seen. He is the Most Gracious, the Most Merciful.*} (59:22)

Is Trinity in the Bible?

Trinity, in contrast, is not in the Bible. The encyclopedias we quoted above state that **the doctrine of Trinity does not exist in the Bible**. They concluded what the questioner concluded that the doctrine was 'developed' in the 4th century.

Trinity doctrine was introduced centuries after the supposed fact. It had to be developed, because it did not exist in the Bible to begin with. The Roman Emperor, Constantine, a pagan, forced his opinion and followed his desire. By cutting the number of gods down to three, he thought it would be more comforting to pagan Europeans rather than making the many gods into only one god, {*"Has he made the âlihah* (gods) (all) *into One Ilâh* (God — Allâh). *Verily, this is a curious thing!"*} (38:5)

Had there been texts from the Bible that answer the question of Trinity, the empire would not have needed councils to develop what is already developed. The questioner agrees to the fact that the doctrine was developed in the 4th century. By doing so, he also agrees that before the 4th century, the doctrine was not developed. This is because it did not exist, as these encyclopaedias assert:

The New Encyclopedia Britannica: "Neither the word Trinity nor the explicit doctrine appears in the New Testament."

The Encyclopedia Americana: "Fourth century Trinitarianism did not reflect accurately early Christian teaching regarding the nature of God; it was, on the contrary, a deviation from this teaching."

The New Catholic Encyclopedia: "The formulation 'one God in three Persons' was not solidly established, certainly not fully assimilated into Christian life and its profession of faith, prior to the end of the 4th century."

Encyclopedia of Religion and Ethics: "In the New Testament we do not find the doctrine of the Trinity in anything like its developed form."

Encyclopedia International: "The doctrine of the Trinity did not form part of the apostles' preaching."

Dictionary of the Bible: "The belief as so defined was reached only in the 4th and 5th centuries AD and hence is not explicitly and formally a biblical belief."

The Oxford Companion to the Bible: "... the developed concept of three coequal partners in the Godhead found in later creedal formulations cannot be clearly detected within the confines of the canon."

These resources, written in plain English by Christians, are not discussing a doctrine that is founded on biblical texts that was later challenged by heretics, and therefore, councils were needed to reaffirm and reassert the old doctrine and the original faith. They speak of a doctrine that mostly did not exist before the 4th century. 'Developed,' is the key word; the questioner agreed to it. It is the truth; can the questioner abide by it?

The questioner equates the description of Allah that is plain, clear and simple and is found in the Quran, the Old Testament and the New Testament, to Trinitarian creed that does not exist in the Bible. Unlike Trinity, there are ample texts that describe Allah's Monotheism in the strict numerical sense throughout the Old Testament, the New Testament and the Quran.

If asked, "Why do you, Muslims, Jews and Christians, believe that Allah is All-Knowledgeable," there would be numerous Texts found in the Old Testament, the New Testament and the Quran that confirm this quality of Allah. In addition, Allah's qualities were preached by the prophets and conform to the general theme that has always prevailed in all three books, that God is One, the One and Only.

In contrast, Trinity does not exist either in the Old Testament or the New Testament. Christians pieced together a creed that was never preached by any prophet nor is found in any text in the Bible. They invented a creed that Jesus and even Paul never spoke of. Because of this massive shortcoming,

Christians always needed to 'glue together' texts that they corrupted and spoiled and made to mean what they do not mean.

Next, the questioner said, "The main stream of Christianity throughout all the world believes in **one God, the Holy Trinity**. It is indeed a mystery, as God Himself is. The incomprehensibility of God is confirmed in the Quran and the Bible. (Job 11:7, 1 Cor 2:11, Surah Al-Anaam 6:103)."

This is typical from Christians. When they are confronted with serious questions about why Trinity, the doctrine, is not found or explained in the Bible, they say, "It is a mystery." Indeed it is. The name of it is not in the Bible. The doctrine of it is not in the Bible. The explanation of it is not in the Bible.

The mainstream of Christianity believes in three different gods, who have three different names, three different personalities, three different roles; two of the three never said they are god. There is a difference between the Old Testament, the New Testament and the Quran pertaining to describing Allah with attributes of perfection, as compared to the invented Trinitarian description of Allah that does not exist in any revealed book. The first type has texts to support it. In contrast, none of these three books spoke of Trinity, whether the name or the doctrine.

Therefore, for the questioner to dodge the real issue about the fact that Trinity the doctrine is not in the Bible, by saying that it is a mystery and that Allah is incomprehensible, proves that Trinity is not in the Bible. If it were, he would have shown humankind the clear text.

To end, we leave the readers with proof that, when quoting the Quran, many Christian evangelicals do not consider the Quran with care. The questioner quoted *ayah* 6:103 to prove Trinity being a mystery, by invoking the incomprehensibility of Allah. Had he read the preceding and the following *ayat*, he would have found that 6:103 rejects Trinity and supports Allah's Islamic Monotheism in the strongest terms, {*Such is Allâh, your Lord! Lâ ilâha illa Huwa* (none has the right to be worshipped but He), *the Creator of all things. So worship Him* (Alone), *and He is the Wakîl* (Trustee, Disposer of affairs or Guardian) *over all things. No vision can grasp Him, but He grasps all vision. He is Al-Latîf* (the Most Subtle and Courteous), *Well-Acquainted with all things. Verily, proofs have come to you from your Lord, so whosoever sees, will do so for* (the good of) *his ownself, and whosoever blinds himself, will do so to his own harm, and I* (Muhammad) *am not a watcher over you.*} (6:102-104)

Peace be on those who follow the true guidance sent to all of Allah's Prophets from Adam to Muhammad, including Noah, Abraham, Moses, and Jesus.

Jalal Abualrub
June 2012

Selected Books Jalal Abualrub Translated or Authored

Madinah Publishers and Distributors (www.islamlife.com)

1) Translated by Jalal Abualrub, edited by Alaa Mencke

❊ Volumes: 1, 2, 3 and 4 of the English Translation of the Encyclopedia of Prophetic Tradition, *Zad-ul Ma`ad fi Hadyi Khairi Al-`Ibad*, by Imam in Qayyim Al-Jauziyyah.

2) Authored by Jalal Abualrub, edited by Alaa Mencke

❊ *Holy Wars, Crusades, Jihad;*

❊ *Biography of Muhammad Ibn Abdul Wahhab;* A 700-page historical study taken from more than 300 different western and Islamic resources on an important part of the history of Arabs in the eighteenth century;

❊ *50 Righteous and Humane Concepts Brought by Muhammad;*

❊ *Muhammad's Role in Islam;*

❊ *The Jewish Temple Rebuilt by the Shi`a;*

❋ *Did Jesus and Muhammad Practice Cross-Dressing;*

❋ *Did Allah Forget the Wives;*

❋ *Length of a Day with Allah;*

❋ *Muslim-Christian Dialogue.*

Books Jalal Abualrub translated for Darussalam Publishers and Distributors (www.dar-us-salam.com)

❋ Chapters (*Juzu*) 1-10, 12, 13, 25-27 of, *Tafsir Ibn Kathir;*

❋ Chapters 1 & 2 of, *Selected Friday Sermons,* (chapters 3 & 4 were translated by Ibrahim Ezghair);

❋ *Pillars of Islam,* by Abdullah Ibn Jabrin;

❋ *Silent Moments,* by Abdul-Malik Al-Qasim;

❋ *How to Achieve Happiness,* by Abdur-Rahman As-Sa`di;

❋ *Healing With the Medicine of the Prophet,* by Imam Ibn Qayyim Al-Jauziyyah;

❋ *The Seerah* (Biography) *of the Prophet,* by Al-Mubarakpuri (Not Published Yet)

❋ *Establish the Prayers & the Prize is Paradise,* by Abdul-Malik Al-Qasim.

Books Jalal Abualrub translated for Dar At-Turath Al-Islami (Dar for Islamic Heritage; Orlando, Florida, USA)

❋ *Innovation, and its Evil Effects,* by Sali'h Al Fozan;
❋ *Rights Basic to the Natural Human Constitution,* by Muhammad Al Uthaymeen;
❋ *The Hadith is Proof Itself in Belief and Laws,* by Nasirudden Al Albani;
❋ *Explaining the Pillars of Iman,* by Mohammad Al Uthaymeen;
❋ *Marriage in Islam,* by Abdurrahman Abdul-Khaliq;
❋ *Kitab Al Ikhlas (Book of Sincerity),* by Husain Al Awaysha;
❋ *Basics & Benefits from the Forty Hadith Nawawi,* by Nathim Sultan.

www.ingramcontent.com/pod-product-compliance
Lightning Source LLC
Chambersburg PA
CBHW071144090426
42736CB00012B/2224